THE REMAINS OF WAR

Apology and Forgiveness

石田甚太ア

JINTARO ISHIDA

THE LYONS PRESS
Guilford, Connecticut
An imprint of The Globe Pequot Press

Originally published in English by Megabooks Company, Quezon City,
Philippines.

Translated from the Japanese by Makiko Okuyama-Ventura, Reynald
Ventura, and Satoshi Masutani
Appendix translated by Bernardino E. Sayo
Project interpreter: Kumiko Anada-Sayo
Editor: Romeo J. Santos

Printed in the United States of America

10 9 8 7 6 5 4 3 2 1

ISBN 1-58574-571-5

The Library of Congress Cataloging-in-Publication Data is available on file.

PROLOGUE

It takes great courage and tenacity to write about a tragic episode in which the writer has participated because the remorse and the sense of having done an unspeakable wrong will continue to fester the writer up to the closing days of his life. Had he not written about it, perhaps the pain and the guilt will not be so searing because the passage of time could have lessened the torture to oneself. In this book *"The Remains of War: Apology and Forgiveness"*, Jintaro Ishida did just that – he gritted his teeth literally and put down on paper the dreariness and the inhumanity of war in which he and his people were the aggressors. Reading through his book, I am reminded of the feelings which the pilot of the bomber Enola Gay experienced when he dropped the atomic bomb on Hiroshima:

> "He knows he will not see the blood
> from the heights from which he flies
> nor can he hear the shrieks
> of dying and of unbearable pain.
>
> But the blood will be there
> etched indelibly, etched indelibly
> not on paper nor on countryside,
> but always burning in him, inside.
>
> This is a point of no return for him –
> he will push the lever, release the bomb,
> then turn away and carry with him
> unspeakable misery – the agony!"

Today, 45 years after the Second World War was ended by the dropping of the atomic bomb on innocent civilians, babies and women, old and young, the sick and the healthy, there is still much pain that one feels about that one act of infamy. If one were to visit the corridors of the United Nations Headquarters in New York City today, he will be able to see some relics of melted stone and scraps of burned flesh whose sights can make the viewer truly sorry for having seen those results of destruction. Such is the agony which Jintaro Ishida had to deal with when he wrote *"The Remains of War: Apology and Forgiveness."*

But then, after undergoing that pain, the experience may well serve as a catharsis for his burned soul, enabling him to breathe more freely and with thanks to the Creator for having given time to reflect and to say "I am truly sorry for everything."

Sedfrey A. Ordoñez

PREFACE

I still have an unanswered question in my mind even after the publication of my book, *Walang Hiya [Without Shame: The Record of Filipino Civilians Massacred by the Japanese Army]* (Tokyo: Gendai-Shokan, 1990). The question was how can I, as a Japanese, answer the Filipino war victims who demand, "We want to know from those Japanese why they tried to kill us?"

I myself wanted to know what those Japanese, who once served the Japanese Imperial Army, now think of what they did some forty-seven years after the War. They massacred Filipino civilians in the name of "guerrilla subjugation."

I located the still living members of the Infantry Regiment and the Airfield Battalion of the Japanese Imperial Army that were stationed in Laguna and Batangas. With some fear and hesitation, I carefully asked them these questions:

1. What is your unforgettable experience in the Philippines?

2. Did you conduct "guerrilla subjugation"? What can you say about the Filipino guerrillas who fought against your Army?

3. Your Army killed many innocent Filipinos. But you claim you only acted in the name of "guerrilla subjugation." How come such killings happened?

4. You visit the Philippines to commemorate the souls of your fallen comrades. Would you also commemorate the souls of those dead Filipinos? Your army turned their land into a battlefield.

5. Do you intend to apologize to Filipino war victims and their country which ruined during the War?

Indeed, I located a hundred Japanese Imperial Army veterans living in different places all over Japan. I called on them without an appointment; I know that it was very impolite of me. I had to do so because they hang up the phone's receiver when I try to make an appointment with them. Thus, I was "an uninvited guest."

I finally finished interviewing the veterans of the Japanese Imperial Army. Armed with their answers to my questions, I went to the Philippines. Then I located their victims – about a hundred of them – during the war. These are the questions I posed to those Filipinos:

1. Some Japanese veterans claim that the soldiers who did the massacre cannot be held responsible. They had to do so because of the order given them by their superiors. What do you think of their reasoning?

2. Some veterans said they conducted "guerrilla subjugation" because the guerrillas attacked them first. What do you think of their justification?

3. Some Japanese veterans claim they had done nothing wrong while they were stationed in the

Philippines. They also claim that when they were charged as war criminals, the decision of the War Tribunal against them was totally wrong. What can you say about it?

4. Japanese veterans now come to the Philippines, which they once turned into a battlefield, to commemorate the souls of their fallen comrades, what can you say about their practice of commemorating only their fallen comrades?

5. Some Japanese soldiers who killed a lot of civilians during the war now wish to apologize to their Filipino war victims and their surviving relatives. Will you accept their apology?

Two years later, I met with the Filipino war victims and their families. They willingly talked to me, so unlike their assailants during the war.

I described the opinions of the assailants and showed these in contrast with those of their victims. I hope that even a thin thread will link them together from the fear and hatred that separated them, they both come from the grassroots of their respective societies.

I fictionalized the names of the Japanese Army veterans. I also did not reveal the names of the military units they had served.

TABLE OF CONTENTS

CHAPTER 4: TAAL, BAUAN

CHAPTER 1

TANAUAN–CALAMBA
HORROR TALES

T he massacre of Filipinos in February and March 1945 in southern Luzon happened because it was ordered by the commander of the Fuji Corps of the Japanese Imperial Army that ruled the area. According to *War History* 60, Army Operation 'Shun' (2), "The Decisive Battle in Luzon" (compiled by the Military History Department in the National Institute for Defense Studies of the Japan Defense Agency), he ordered the "guerrilla containment" or guerrilla subjugation through the following circumstances:

> *The corps commander held a meeting with the officers at the rank not less than company commander on January 25, 1945, immediately after he had received a report. The report said that a pacification company under his order had suffered approximately ten deaths and injuries in the San Pablo area in the middle of January and that a battalion suffered another death and injuries amounting to more than ten soldiers in various areas around the 22nd of the same month. And he ordered to 'pacify the guerrillas right now before the battle against the U.S. Army.' He said, 'Assume the residents as guerrillas and pacify them if they cooperate with guerrillas. I will assume all responsibility as corps commander.' The corps pacified the residents by following this order.*

The background of this order was that the Japanese Army had been forced to fight against both the U.S. Army coming from the front and the guerrillas, attacking from the back, in January 1945 when the U.S. Army landed on Lingayen Bay in Luzon. Based on its bitter experience described above, the headquarters of the X Area Army gave the following instruction to the Fuji Corps not as an order but as an advice:

Before we start to fight the American forces, we must make sure that the back and the surroundings of our troops are uninhabitable [by the enemy, residents, and guerrillas].

In Calamba, the hometown of Jose Rizal, the national hero of the Philippines, there is a memorial erected near the site of a mass slaughter in Barangay Real. It said in Filipino language that the Japanese Army killed two thousand men there.

The memorial in Barangay Real, Calamba

(On February 12, 1945, in this barangay, two thousand men were deceived and gathered here from Calamba, Laguna. They were tied and slaughtered with bayonets without reason.)

November 1, 1965
Calamba Lions Club

The Japanese Army herded the men living in the barrio to the town's Catholic church, brought them to the suburb by trucks, and then massacred them in the name of "guerrilla subjugation." Mainly the X Company of the X Infantry Regiment conducted this "Calamba guerrilla subjugation." Some soldiers of the Engineer Company of this regiment and the X Company of the X Amphibious Base Battalion also participated in it.

Masao Yokoyama: Fighting for My Family and Nation

I got off at a station near the Sea of Japan, but there was no smell of sea. When I told Masao Yokoyama that I wanted to ask about his war experience in the Philippines, his fat and healthy face frowned.

"Since I was not an officer, I have nothing to talk about . . . In fact, I do not want to talk about it," he said.

But when I ask him safe or harmless questions, he started talking. He was not so eager to talk. He stood upright at his doorstep.

"What is your unforgettable experience during the war?" I asked.

5

"The fact that I survived miraculously. While we were fighting a losing battle, I suffered four injuries and could not walk well. When we withdrew, our company commander ordered us to leave those severely injured and those who cannot walk, myself included. I walked desperately with them with the aid of a stick, hoping to survive. By allowing me to walk with them, I was saved.

"I served for five years in Manchuria and the Philippines. I was qualified to receive a pension. The length of our military service is tripled for the service we have rendered during a war when they finally calculate the duration of our service. But I simply declined to receive it. I was happy just because I had been saved and been able to go back to Japan. I hope they would give my pension to the families of those who were killed in the war.

"By the way, I recently received a letter from my grandson's young teacher. He asked, 'For what reason did you fight in the war?' I wrote, 'I fought to defend the Japanese people, my family and the nation.'

"But your unit killed as many as 2,000 Filipinos in Calamba, didn't it?" I asked.

"They say we killed *that* many people? That's as many as one division. It may be only 100 or 150 persons. Like in the case of the Nanking Massacre, they were just exaggerating," he said.

"Don't you remember? Your unit gathered the men of the town and, herded them to the church in Calamba. Then they were brought to the suburb by trucks to be killed. It was conducted in the name of "guerrilla subjugation." But actually it was meant to kill all the men of the town," I said.

He looked down and said nothing. His face began to turn red and it looked as if he was going to shout any moment. He finally spoke after a long silence. "I am sorry. I understand that you have come a long way to see me. But I do not want to talk on that subject," he said.

He saw me off at the main street.

"I made a list of my comrades who had been killed in the war. I am sending them to those who survived; I hope they can pray for the souls of our comrades even only at sunrise and sunset," he said.

"Would you mind if I ask you to pray also for the souls of your Filipino war victims? You can do it by adding only one line on your list," I said.

He looked at me perplexed.

Daizaburo Ohara: Hemp Ropes and Nightmares

Weak autumn rains were continuously falling as if they had already stopped. When I came to Daizaburo Ohara's house in a rice field near a small hill, his wife is watching television. She told me he is still working because he is still healthy.

I visited him in his work place. He works in the maintenance department of a building. When he had finished his day's work, we talked at the end of a passageway.

"What can you tell me about the war in the Philippines?" I asked.

"You want to know about the 'guerrilla subjugation,' because you ask me about the war in the Philippines," he began talking while his eyes were fixed downward.

"I kill everyday, as if I was not satisfied having killed that many. I hate doing it before, during, and after. But I have no choice because I was ordered to do so . . ."

"In Calamba, they were brought fast by trucks. We could not use our bayonets to kill that many people. So, we strangled them with hemp ropes. I will wound a hemp rope twice round the neck of a victim, and put my knee on his back. Then I will pull the rope backward strongly to choke him to death. We never failed to kill in this way. We killed even women and children in this method. I thought that it was not necessary to kill those children so when I remember that massacre, I feel very sorry for them. I cannot sleep with my feet pointing to the direction of the Philippines," he said.

"Have you attended a memorial service for your fallen comrades in the Philippines?" I asked.

"I have not gone there since the war. When I think about the fact that I killed Filipinos everyday, I do not want to go there just to pray for the souls of my comrades. I do not want to attend even our veterans' gathering," he said.

"I'm having nightmares even now. I had one only the other day. In it I was killed with a gun and bayonet. In early years, it was nightmares in which Filipinos killed me. Recently American soldiers killed me. I believe that I have such nightmares because I had killed many people at the front. I cry and wake up every time I had such a nightmare." He wiped his thick and stout neck with his big hand as if to remove his sweat.

"We are now living in a peaceful time. But I sometimes doubt whether it is all right when I think of what we did during the war. My heart is filled with the feeling of penitence, though this feeling cannot be called (as exaggerated) as expiation."

"I cannot endure it in my mind if I think of the past too much. So I consulted with two of my brothers when we met. And I decided not to talk about what happened during the war. Three of us went to fronts and returned unharmed. I am willing to apologize but I hope the Japanese government should make the apology, not the individual veteran.

"We suffered very much because our unit always stayed out front. Many of my comrades were killed. Because I was of low rank, I always get kicked and slapped. Sometimes when I look up at the night sky, I even wished that I were killed just with the shot of one bullet. I envied my dead comrades," he said.

When we had finished our conversation, I saw his yellow T-shirt stained with sweat.

Shozo Sato: Menaced by Guerrillas

It was difficult to find Shozo Sato's house because his nameplate was not clearly printed. He lives in a small two-story prefabricated house.

Later, someone guided me into a room floored with tatami-mats. Then Sato-san arrived. Even after I had handed him my calling card and introduced myself, he remained sitting in a formal way. He was one of the leaders of the main force responsible for the "guerrilla subjugation" in Calamba.

"When I look back at those times, I think I made some foolish mistakes. I became a soldier without knowing what an army is. Because I was born to a poor family, I hoped to enter a school in which my tuition would be covered with government subsidy. My parents also admired soldiers, saying that they are disciplined," he said.

"Weren't you convicted as a war criminal there [Philippines]?" I asked.

According to *The Documents on B and C Class War Criminals by the Tribunals in Manila (as conducted by the) U.S. Forces* published by Fuji Shuppan, four officials and soldiers, including him, were sentenced to thirty years imprisonment or death by hanging.

"The military police stationed near Calamba Church at the time reported that the guerrilla movement was becoming active. Based on this report, we were dispatched from the corps headquarters in Tanauan. I was ordered to 'subjugate the guerrillas'. I believe I did not kill innocent Filipinos," he said.

"In the church where the Filipinos were herded, did you check whether or not they were guerrillas?" I asked.

"No. Because I received a report from the military police, and because it was difficult to investigate . . ." he said.

"That's a self-serving reason. If you consider the view of the Filipinos, they could not take that they were killed merely because they were suspected as guerrillas and without any investigation. What can you say to that?" I asked.

"We had no time to do so . . ." he said.

"But you have not fought a battle yet. U.S. Forces have yet to land in Batangas and have not approached from Manila. It was only February 12, 1945," I said.

"Two days before, five of our comrades, including a company commander, were killed in an ambush by guerrillas. The commander served for a long time in the Army and even fought in Manchuria with us. We were in an atmosphere of menace," he said.

"Do you mean to say you killed them to avenge your five comrades? Though the Japanese were

11

invading other countries, do you think they were permitted to kill thousands of Filipinos forcibly? Do you think those Filipinos will accept your reasoning?" I asked.

"I also had a doubt on why we had to kill them. Once I even ordered to stop the killing while we're in the middle of executions without consulting anybody. I think I lost my will," he said.

"You say you subjugated them because they were guerrillas. What do you think of their guerrilla movement at the time?" I asked.

"I think their guerrilla movement is a bad combat tactic," he said.

"Why did the Filipinos resist the Japanese Army even if doing so would endanger their lives? Even though you had powerful weapons?" I asked.

"I cannot answer you right now," he said.

"Reverse the situation. Suppose the Philippines invades Japan, deprive us of food, and slap, torture, and even kill our countrymen, alleging that we are guerrillas. Do you think we the Japanese will just be silent?" I asked.

"Had I been younger, I could do more substantial things . . . Anyway, we have done some wrong to the Filipinos. We must not forget that. I am thinking of doing something before I leave this world. What should it be?

"Recently, one of my former subordinates sent me a list of our fallen comrades. I put that list before our family altar so I can pray for their souls," he said.

That list must have been copied from somewhere and sent to him by Yokoyama-san who lives in northern Japan. I asked him to add the line—"War victims in the Philippines"—at the end of the list and to remember it whenever he prays. He nodded in agreement.

Motoichi Tanabe: If I were a Young Filipino, I would be a Guerrilla

The cold north wind blows as if it wants to fan the rice paddies under a cloudy sky.

Mr. and Mrs. Motoichi Tanabe were in the farm, helping one of their relatives in the harvesting. I arrived just in time for their afternoon break. I approached Tanabe-san who is sitting on bundles of straw piled at one side of the farm road.

"We were ordered to retreat to Mt. Banahaw from a cave in Mt. Malipuyo. We had to move after giving a hand grenade each to those who could not walk, so they could kill themselves with it. It was a pity to leave our wounded comrades behind, because they asked us to help them," he said.

"Did you have a part in the subjugation in Calamba?" I asked.

"I was on duty in the corps headquarters at the time . . .," he said in a low voice and averted his eyes.

"From your comrades who had a part in a subjugation, did you learn of those incidents that happen every day?" I asked.

"After one such incident, we did not talk about it even among our close comrades. I heard that it happened, but they kept silent. I heard later that they had been very busy because trucks kept arriving one after another, bringing captives. They had to kill all of them before the next truck arrives," he said.

He lighted a cigarette and puffed the smoke hesitantly.

"Have you gone to the Philippines for a memorial service?" I asked.

"No, I haven't been there since the war. It was hell. I hate to go there at any rate. Nothing good to remember there at all. It was truly a living hell. If I visit the Philippines, I would only recall bad memories and suffer.

"Several years ago, a major newspaper had an article on a Filipino who was a victim of guerrilla subjugation. I hid it so that my family could not read it. This topic is taboo for me. I want to forget everything. When I recall it, I know that we committed dreadful acts. We stole food and crops. We killed men. It was reasonable that they acted against us Japanese. If I were a young Filipino, I surely would be a guerrilla fighter."

I continued to listen.

"Let me tell you another story: Several years ago, we took a trip to a spring in Yamagata. That night, I went to a place in town with two of my friends. A Filipina entertainer served us. I carelessly told her that I was stationed in southern Luzon when I was a soldier. She said that the Japanese Imperial Army killed some of her relatives. After hearing her say that, I could not stay there anymore. I went out from there as if I want to run away. It is really difficult for me to talk about the Philippines. I do not want to talk about it, as much as possible. I am sorry you came a long way just to interview me," he said while pulling grass stalks from the ground one by one.

Tadao Yoshikawa: War and Rumor of a Burning

Tadao Yoshikawa's hand was shot as he retreated from Mt. Malipuyo. He talked hesitantly while looking down.

"Our company was always placed in the front line; we suffered a lot. Our company commander was insane with anger. He felt greatly responsible because his soldiers were getting killed in one battle after another," he said.

"What's your role in the guerrilla subjugation in Calamba?" I asked. Yoshikawa-san's mouth twitched right away.

"Why ask me such a question? I can't remember. The tropical atmosphere was hot. I was too lazy to remember. I tried to forget it. I don't want to recall it. I don't want to talk about it," he said with a stiff face.

"How did you feel when you were caught?" I asked.

"When I became a POW (prisoner of war)? I felt nothing in particular. I was not joyous when the war ended. A rumor went around that we would be brought to an uninhabited island and burned with a firebomb. I was uncertain. I didn't believe it, though.

"My comrades told me to keep my distance from them because my wound smelled and its pus attracted flies. I was embittered because they had made me work hard and became cruel to me when I was injured.

"I was admitted to a field hospital of the U.S. Army. American army surgeons are gentlemen. They are not arrogant, so unlike Japanese doctors. I observed this difference clearly.

"When I returned to Japan, I was admitted to a hospital and my wounded right hand was operated on because it greatly swelled. It suffered a compound fracture and small pieces of bone stuck into the flesh," he said.

"Do you know that there are still many survivors of the war in the Philippines who were attacked by the Japanese? I am sorry for them. But I heard that Filipinos can even cure stomachache just by taking toothpaste with water because they seldom take medicine . . .," he said.

"By the way, you took part in the guerrilla subjugation in Taal, didn't you? Although you belonged to a corps different from ours," Yamada-san said to Yoshikawa-san. He is a comrade of Yoshikawa-san. He brought me here by his car.

Yoshikawa-san said: "We set fire on houses in the village near Taal Lake in the beginning. Then we shot the people with machine guns and rifles when they ran out of their houses.

"In war, might is right. After Japan surrendered without any condition, we had no chance to complain. We were tried as vicious one-sidedly.

"When we surrendered, Filipinos shouted at us 'Bakayaro, Dorobo Patay,'" he said

"Why did Filipinos abuse you?" I asked.

"Perhaps because we stole their food," he said.

"You must have done more than just stealing," I said.

"Do you think that we did more than that? In the battlefield, I was ready to die each day. I believed that my death would not be meaningless. I fought hard because I want to be memorialized in the Yasukuni Shrine in case I get killed. I did nothing to be blamed."

"Do you regret having made the Philippines a battlefield?" I asked.

"I do not have such a feeling at all. We could not avoid it because it was war," he said.

17

Masaharu Ueda: Fighting in a Foreign Land

Masaharu Ueda lives in a high-rise apartment building with a splendid view. He was an officer and had a stout dark face.

"Somebody said the guerrilla activity had become rampant in the Philippines because Japan's occupation policy failed or because of the misconduct of the Japanese Imperial Army. But I did not commit any wrongdoing. I used military currency properly when I bought food," he said.

"You still think you did not commit any wrongdoing?" I asked.

"Yes, I do. Why do you ask?" he said.

"It is because the military currency was worthless. According to Filipinos, they refused to sell goods for military currency in the last period of the war. They even called it Mickey Mouse money or toy money. Because its value deteriorated and resulted in inflation, they had to pay 300 pesos even for a cup of coffee," I explained.

"But they sold goods to the Japanese Imperial Army for military currency," he said.

"Ueda-san, did you go out for food procurement?" I asked.

"No, I didn't. I was an officer."

"It was not a trade, but they went out for procurement by carrying a gun. In reality, it was a plundering if we call it flatly," I said.

"One day, the *tiniente del barrio* came. He was angry, saying that the Japanese Imperial Army had stolen their vegetables. We gathered my soldiers for him to identify the thieves But he could not find them. We asked the permission of the captain of another company for him to identify other soldiers. The tiniente del barrio found the thieves from his company. I slapped some twenty soldiers.

"But I could not make friends with Filipinos. Or maybe I could not like them. They were suspicious, hedonistic, and not willing to work; perhaps because they were placed under a colonial rule for a long time. While we were powerful, they followed us. But when we could not give anything because of lack of resources, they sided with the Americans who gave them commodities. They lacked a sense of patriotism and just acted for their own gain. I could not like them," he said.

"If we limit the discussion to the last period of the war, the Japanese Army had ordered to kill all Filipinos while the Americans sent the wounded Filipinos to their field hospitals for them to be saved. Filipinos escaped to the area occupied by the American Army to save themselves. Do you consider it as a change of heart?" I asked.

But he was not interested in my argument.

"I remember now that we built our position in the potato fields of the farmers. We enclosed the area with barbed wires. Though the farmers living in the vicinity owned the field, other units warned the farmers that they would shoot the farmers if they would enter the field. But my unit guaranteed that they could freely enter the field to harvest their potatoes," he said.

He looked at me with a smiling face. He looked satisfied for having recalled an episode in which he acted as a kind officer.

"How do you feel now having gone through the battlefield in the Philippines?" I asked.

"I hope we must not make Japan a battlefield. Though I was an officer, I did not fight for the Emperor. I fought in a foreign country to defend the Japanese people who stayed behind. I believe that we should only fight in a foreign land if we have to fight," he said.

"Do you believe so because you saw how horrible it was when towns and villages were burned and many people were killed in the Philippines?" I asked.

"Yes. It was terrible. I don't want to remember that scene," he said.

Mario Lantakong: Present at the Massacre Site

I rode a bus going to San Pablo from Plaza Lawton in Manila and got off at the center of Calamba, Laguna. Then, I rode a jeepney and tricycle to enter Barangay Aplaya. I had visited this barangay in 1989.

After two years of interval, I hoped that I could see the Ancalas and Mambakas whom I met previously. I could not interview them then because they are not well at the time.

I called several old men who were drinking beer and chatting on a verandah. One of them was Mario Lantakong. He returned to the Philippines from America about a month earlier and was scheduled to go back to the United States the following day. He worked as a machine mechanic when he emigrated to the U.S. in 1979. And he had retired, as he was already sixty-seven years old then.

"I was twenty years old then. The Japanese Army surrounded our barangay and summoned all the male residents in the houses. Because Salo, a female member of Makapili (Organization of Japanese collaborators established on December 8, 1944), said that 'they are going to ask us to do a special work'. We were gathered at an elementary school; we brought our lunch. After that they ordered us to walk to a church to gather there. All of us were males. We were accompanied by several Japanese soldiers with rifles," he spoke fast in English.

"Without any investigation in the church, we were brought to the massacre site at once by a truck. Japanese soldiers took our lunch and threw them on the way. When we arrived in Real, we were shut up in a house with an elevated floor.

"At around 12 p.m., the massacre began. When I saw that the others were being killed with bayonets, I ran away desperately because I hate to be killed in such a painful way. I heard what sounded like gunshot but I ran away for my life. I was lucky because I was just injured here but was not killed," he said.

He showed me a wound by rolling up a sleeve of his T-shirt. A bullet had entered his body from the backside of his left shoulder and went through to the front.

"The guerrillas were the enemy for the Japanese Imperial Army. But they could not identify who is a guerrilla. So, they tried to kill all the men in Calamba," I said.

The Catholic church in Calamba where the victims were herded and later massacred.

"Is that what they said? It is a selfish reasoning. Those victims could not accept such a reasoning," he replied.

"Some Japanese said they had no responsibility because they had to kill Filipinos because of the order given them," I said.

"Unbelievable. Both of them are responsible. Those who ordered it and those who killed with bayonets. I do not want to listen to such an excuse. How irresponsible the Japanese are!" he said.

"Any message to the Japanese?" I asked.

"I am still angry at them. I may go crazy when they say such a useless excuse even though they killed old men, women, and even children. I will never forget what the Japanese did. I hated the Japanese since then.

"Because I am a Christian, I want to forgive the Japanese. But the Japanese killed us, Filipinos, the children of God, for their own selfish reasons. I want you to think of it seriously," he said.

"Any message for those young Japanese who did not experience the war?" I asked.

"I hope that you will never repeat what your grandfathers did. Never," he said.

"How do you feel about coming back to the Philippines after quite an interval?" I asked.

"My homeland is a good place; it is where I was born. I enjoy its nice food and am familiar with its language. I have friends to talk to; we can drink beer together. I love the Philippines," he said.

Juanita Adesas: My Father should have been killed in an instant

I went to Barangay Pansol by Laguna de Bay at the outskirts of Calamba. It was my second visit to Mrs. Sebastian Adesas. Her house is located beside the railroad-track that runs from Manila to Bicol.

"The victims in my family was my husband and second daughter. My husband's hands were tied behind him and he was stabbed once from behind with a bayonet. His wound was very deep, and the bayonet pierced through his chest and even reached his foot. It was a terrible wound," she said.

Juanita, Mrs. Adesas's second daughter, came back home after washing clothes in the river. She does the laundry of a family of eight persons and is paid seven hundred pesos a month. But because she could not support her family only through this, her daughter augments their earning by working as a stay-in maid. She was injured at the buttocks in the massacre in which her father was killed.

"Is it true that some Japanese claim that the Japanese soldiers are not responsible for the victims of war in the Philippines and that it is not necessary to apologize because the guerrillas were the enemy of the Japanese Army and fought on equal terms?" she asked. I nodded.

"I hate to listen to such an opinion by the Japanese. If they neglect the victims, why did they invade this country? If the Japanese had not come here, such a cruel incident would not have happened. For those Japanese who want to apologize to the victims of war, I will forgive them for what they had committed in the past. It is because the war happened a long time ago. But I do not forgive those who claim that they need not apologize. I hate war very much. I hope that both those former soldiers and the young generation of Japanese must not fight a war and invade another country anymore. I am already fifty-six years old and very weak. If the Japanese wish to help us, I am ready to accept help even from them, even from those who tried to kill us. Please tell them," she said.

I then pointed a microphone to her sister who kept listening to us. She was almost killed by fragments of shells by the U.S. Forces when she was about three or four months old.

"I want to say to the young Japanese that I hate discrimination among people. The Japanese are like animals during the war but I hope that the young Japanese will join hands with us. I want to deepen my friendship with the young Japanese as persons," she said.

"Did you have any experience of discrimination by the Japanese?" I asked.

"No, I didn't have. They say that it was rampant during the war. Was it possible for them to tie up the hands of my father and to stab him with a bayonet as forcefully as possible, if the Japanese had not discriminated Filipinos. I don't want them to do such a thing again. I hope they treat us equally," she said.

Guided by Juanita, I went to the house of Mrs. Quebas who wasn't there when we called on her. Her eldest son had died six months earlier due to a lung disease. He was my guide in my previous visit.

While we were walking a winding narrow path under a burning sun, Juanita said this, as if to herself:

"It would have been better for my father if he had been killed instantly. He became weaker and weaker because we could not find food during that period. He died in pain a year after he was stabbed by a soldier of the Japanese Imperial Army."

Lope Mendoza: A Commemoration Every February 22nd

From Calamba, Laguna I went to Tanauan, Batangas. In a crowded market, I found a jeepney going to Barangay Birong-Biron. The jeepney was filled to overflowing with women and their groceries, but I managed to get in.

The jeepney, swinging left to right, made a cloud of dust as it ran slowly on a bumpy road.

Lope Mendoza was not home; he was out in the field. I remember he had offered me big ripe mangoes because it was mango harvesting season when I first met him.

He was left for dead by the Japanese Imperial Army on the night he was forced to bring a load up the mountain with other men from his barangay.

He survived even though he was stabbed with a bayonet with both his hands tied at the back. But his father was killed there. When he returned to the village the following day, he found out that even their women and children had been killed. And their houses had been burned down.

Thirty-seven men were brought to the mountain, but only five men returned. Three men among them died later and only two of those men are alive today.

I greeted him for our reunion when he returned from the field and came into the living room after changing into a clean shirt. He looked almost the same even after an interval of two years.

"Do you want to know what we do during the commemoration ceremony?" he asked.

I learned from his wife that they hold a commemoration ceremony every year on February 22nd, the day when the massacre happened. I asked about it again.

"It is a day for me to thank God because it was the day when I survived. Because this place is too far for the parish priest to come from his church in the town, we ask the lay leader to lead the prayer. It is a day to comfort the souls of those killed and to thank God for my survival.

"On that day, the family members of the victims gather in my house to drink, eat, and chat. It is a cheerful day," he said.

"The Japanese say they killed Filipinos to fight against the guerrillas," I told him.

"I will never agree with such a self-serving opinion. Why did they kill even babies? The following day after we were stabbed, the Japanese Imperial Army attacked this barrio. They massacred more than seventy women and children and set fire on the houses. I cannot understand why they claim so while they killed innocent children. I was fourteen years old then, but those children younger than me were killed, too. They did not resist the Japanese Imperial Army and they were innocent. The Japanese must be held responsible for what they say because they killed the people in this country," he said.

"Do you have anything to say to the Japanese?" I asked.

"If those soldiers involved in the massacre of the residents in this village are still alive, I want them to extend kind assistance to those victims of war, like us. I hope they show good faith as Japanese who have made mistakes in this barangay, not as the government of Japan," he said.

"You should demand it not from the individual person but from the Japanese government, because the most responsible for the invasion of this country was the Japanese government. Although the Japanese are believed to be rich, the individual Japanese, like me, is not so rich," I said.

"You must be rich because you came to the Philippines by airplane," he replied.

I smiled wryly in spite of myself.

When we were waiting for a jeepney by the roadside to return to the hotel in Los Baños, Laguna, Lope Mendoza came out and told me an unexpected tale.

"During the last days of the war, a member of the Makapili lives in this barrio. He works for the Japanese Imperial Army and told on everyone who is a guerrilla when the Japanese Imperial Army attacked this barrio. The village folks were so angry at him that they punched him to death after the Japanese Imperial Army surrendered. But his wife and children were allowed to escape in the night because unlike him, they were not members of the Makapili," he said.

Makapili became synonymous to "spies for the Japanese." Its members are still being blamed today as they betrayed their compatriots for the gains of the Japanese Imperial Army.

Constancio Derna: I Held My Thirst

I met with Constancio Derna in Barangay San Juan for the first time. He was thin like a dead tree. His shoulders were bent low for he had been stabbed three times on his upper body with a bayonet and one of those stabs pierced through his body from the chest to the back. Since we belong to the same generation, as a Japanese who is as old as he is, I could not help but apologize to him before the interview.

"It was about six in the morning. I was drinking a cup of coffee, when Japanese soldiers went to the houses and gathered us in a house near the railroad crossing. They forced us to walk to the Calamba Catholic Church around eleven in the morning. The church was full of men. At around two in the afternoon, we were brought to the massacre site in Barangay Real by truck."

"Before they brought us, a Makapili and Japanese soldiers checked if we were carrying a pass issued by the Japanese Army. Those who had the pass were released. Only those who collaborated with the Japanese Imperial Army had the pass. Because we were ordinary residents and collaborated neither with the Japanese nor the Americans, we did not carry a pass.

"When the truck arrived at Real, the Japanese soldiers tied our hands at the back and covered our eyes. Then they pushed us into a house. Those brought to the ground floor were the first to be killed. I lost consciousness after I was stabbed three times on my chest. I think they killed those brought up to the second floor when the ground floor was already filled with dead bodies. When I regained consciousness, I felt thirsty very much. I drank the liquid that dripped down from the second floor. Perhaps it was the blood of those killed.

"Then, I lost consciousness again. I could not recall how long I was down. But when I regained consciousness, I found out there was another survivor. Because the Japanese soldiers were checking if we were still alive, we pretended to be dead. When the soldiers were gone, that man and I helped each other untie ourselves. Then, I lost consciousness again. Sometime later, I crawled from the house to the bank of a river. I looked back and saw the house was burning with those dead bodies.

"The following day, I found the man dead at the river's edge. Perhaps he died because he drank the water in the river. I held my thirst. I think I survived because I did not drink that water. Guerrillas happened to pass by and they brought me to their field hospital in Canlubang. But because the Japanese Army attacked the hospital, we had to evacuate. I could not get out from bed; I thought I will die there. But the residents helped me. I met my sister in Barrio Santa Rosa and asked her to tell our parents that I'm still alive. Eleven men survived from the massacre among sixty-seven men who were brought out from my barrio. I am the only survivor now.

"It took more than a year before my wounds healed completely. Actually my body hasn't returned to its normal form. I could not do hard manual labor since then. Because the nerve in my chest was cut by a bayonet, my doctor prohibited me from doing hard work. I have the support of my brothers and sisters; but still I live like a beggar. My wife earns a little by washing other people's clothes," he said.

"According to the Japanese who participated in the Calamba massacre, they gathered and killed the men because they received a notice from the military police in Calamba saying that the residents acted doubtfully . . .," I said.

"What do you mean by 'acted doubtfully'?" he asked.

"It means, for example, the residents collaborated with the guerrillas or they had some conspiracy against Japan," I said.

"That's wrong. There was no guerrilla member and there was no such a movement. Why did they try to kill us? I want to know the reason," he said.

"Any message to those Japanese soldiers who are still alive?" I asked.

"I wish they will help those who could not work since then like me," he said.

His son-in-law was listening eagerly to us. He has a mustache and fair complexion. I asked for his opinion.

He thrust his body forward to me. "The war was fought between Japan and the United States, but Japan invaded the Philippines. The victims of the war like my father-in-law are still suffering. He could not work since he was wounded in the massacre. Is it possible to make an arrangement so that I can work in Japan to help my father-in-law who was wounded by the

Japanese Imperial Army and is still suffering now?" he said.

Casiano Reblo: Even Children were Guerrilla Fighters?

I crossed a simple bridge made of logs of coconut trees and covered with wood boards, I was careful not to fall off. The space under the bridge was being used as a garbage dump and the garbage that had piled up smelled.

Casiano Reblo of Barangay Samperohan has had a stroke. He has moved to his daughter's house so she could take care of him.

When I opened a wooden door after calling him, I saw that he lay on a wooden bed on the floor of the house. At a glance, I concluded he was sick and was discouraged. But the power in his voice still remains when we started talking.

"Because I was an adult and could fight the Japanese, they could kill me if they suspect me of being a guerrilla. But why did they kill children who could not even walk. They attacked and killed two of my children, wife, and twelve-year-old sister. One of my children was less than a year old and the other was only two. When they noticed that Japanese soldiers were coming, they tried to escape. But they were shot at the back. Why did they kill even my children?" he said.

Did the Japanese consider even children were guerrilla fighters? Do you believe that? What did my children do to them? Did they help the guerrillas even though they could not speak yet? Please don't be foolish. How did the Japanese come to such a convenient reason after they had killed my children?" he stared at me pointedly.

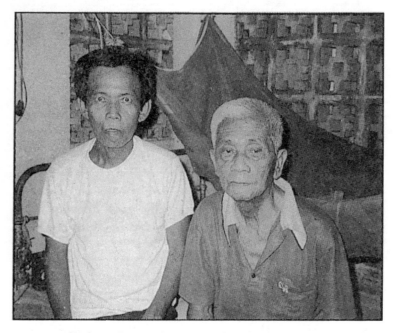

Casiano Reblo (right) of Barangay Samperohan, Calamba and his son (left).

"Filipinos became guerrillas because the Japanese treated us like animals. We did not have good weapons and thus endangered our lives. The Japanese slapped us and forced us to bow down. Slapping is humiliates Filipinos tremendously. And they raped our women, took our food by force, tortured and killed suspects without any investigation. If you were treated like that, can you remain silent?

"The Japanese used the Makapili. This tactic created disintegration among Filipinos. They used them as spies to arrest guerrillas and suspected guerrillas. But, of course, we sympathized with the guerrillas rather than the Makapili who sold us, their compatriots.

"In those days, the Philippines was a colony of the United States. But we were more democratic than the Japanese under the emperor system. We were repelled by the Japanese because they destroyed the colonial system and tried to rule us, Japanese – style. We were rather familiar with the American way. And then the Japanese Army arrested us at random to torture and kill us. I was arrested thrice. If the Makapili hated me, I would have been tortured and killed even though I am not a guerrilla.

"When the Japanese Army began the Occupation, we did not think they were an invading force, because they claimed they are planning to build the East Asia Common Prosperity Area. We also believed they are 'tomodachi' (friend). When we noticed that what they are doing is different from what they are saying, we realized that their claims are mere propaganda; we opposed them secretly in our mind. We kept silent because we feared the Japanese Army. But we already realized that they came here to invade us and make the Philippines a colony of Japan. Then, we rebelled against them," he said.

"What will you do if the Japanese come here to apologize?" I asked.

"I will accept them because I am democratic. I am also a Christian who believes in God. But I would not have forgiven them if they had come here right after Liberation. But it has been a long time since then.

"Are the Japanese still distressed about the fact that they killed Filipinos? Are they just bearing up without telling the truth to their wives and children? Perhaps they regret what they did. I hope they really regret it and repent. I want to pray so that such an incident will not happen again.

"Soon, we will hold the anniversary of the massacre. As you know, it is on February 12. We had collected and buried the bones under the memorial in front of my house. We could not identify the remains because they had been burned. My wife, children, and sister rest there, too," he said.

When I came out of his house, I saw the white column-shaped memorial in a small plaza in front of his house. Its marker in Filipino said:

Including innocent children, adults, pregnant women and even infants held by their mothers, seventy residents were stabbed with a bayonet and burned to death.

Buenaventura Gregoria: We Remember even if We Forgive

Buenaventura Gregoria testified about his war experience before Japanese audiences, when he was invited to Japan by a people's organization, the Forum to Reflect upon War Victims in the Asia-Pacific Region and Engrave It in Our Minds years ago. When I visited him in his village, he has just been elected as a barangay captain of Barangay Samperohan in the elections of 1989.

"Was it the policy of the Japanese Imperial Army to kill and burn Filipinos indiscriminately as it did in Calamba? I think the worst thing the Japanese Army had done is to arrest those suspected of being guerrillas by using the Makapili. Just think how the Japanese would act, if the army of another country invaded Japan and did the same.

"Compared with the Japanese Army, the U.S. Forces were kind to us. The Japanese Army massacred people in Calamba, but the Americans treated us in their field hospital at once when they found out we were wounded. This difference was that between the killer and the angel."

"Do you know there some former Japanese soldiers who want to apologize?" I asked.

"I think they are those Japanese who have a conscience, will not have tormented and killed others for no reason. I am happy to know that . . ." he said.

He continued: "Because I am a Catholic, I love even those Japanese who were once our enemies. Because I believe in the love of God, I am willing to welcome those Japanese who regret what they have done and sincerely apologize.

"I hope they will support us in return as much as possible because the Philippines is now in an economic crisis," he said.

"Will you forgive the Japanese who killed your family?" I asked.

"It will be difficult to do so . . . I want to welcome them. But I will not be able to become a true friend when I recall that my mother, brothers, and a sister had been their victims. We may shake hands, but I will have some mixed feelings in my mind. I may pretend to welcome them. I may not be able to hold their hands firmly," he said.

I asked him: "Do you know the Japanese hide the fact that they have committed massacres in the Philippines and are trying to forget them?"

"Unlike them, we hold a ceremony on the day of the massacre to commemorate the incident every year so as not to forget, even though we forgive the war crimes committed by the Japanese," he said.

"What happens on February 12?" I asked.

"On the commemoration day of February 12 each year, we hold a mass for the souls of those killed. The children offer flowers and we hold a parade in the afternoon. In the procession, high school students assume the role of the Japanese. They hit and torture the people. It is reenacted so that the youth will not forget the massacre. We hope that such a massacre will not happen again in any country," he said.

Lastly, I asked: "What's your problem in this barangay?"

"We should repair the bridge immediately, but the budget is not enough for it. The unemployment of the youth is also a big problem. Seventy percent of the youth is jobless. Some of them indulge in drugs because they have lost hope. A major problem is the Calabarzon project. It is meant to industrialize Cavite, Laguna, Batangas, and Quezon provinces through funding from Japan. Though it might not affect this region, the angry farmers in Cavite and Batangas are holding a campaign against the project, claiming that Marubeni is buying up all farm lands," he said.

"What about the pollution of Laguna de Bay?" I asked.

"Fish catch is steadily decreasing for fifteen years now. My son is a fisherman, but he must change his job if the number of factories increases further in this region. I hope a Japanese factory will hire him, if he has to give up fishing. As a barangay captain, I am afraid that trouble might erupt between the government and the people's organizations. The government plans to build big industrial estates through investments from foreign countries but these organizations oppose that plan," he said.

CHAPTER 2

LOS BAÑOS, BAI, AND SAN PABLO

A ccording to the *"Japanese Army War Crime Record"* which is kept in the archives of The National Library (TNL) of the Philippines, about 600 residents were massacred from February 21 to March 6, 1945 in Los Baños, an adjoining town of Calamba, in Laguna.

In the *X Infantry, X Regiment Philippine Islands War History"* a "guerrilla subjugation" in Bai, an adjoining town of Los Baños, was reported thus:

> *On February 6, (1945), the guerrillas attacked and killed Mr. Kobayashi, an apprentice finance officer (in Bai). On February 9, we the 116th Battalion subjugated the guerrillas around Bai.*

The 116th Battalion means the X Amphibious Base Battalion. Bai was considered as guerrilla territory by the Japanese Army then. This subjugation was conducted in three places: (1) Bai, (2) Los Baños, and (3) San Pablo.

In San Pablo, 600 Chinese and about 70 Filipinos, who were suspected as guerrillas were massacred on February 24. A splendid memorial was erected in the Chinese cemetery and the details of the massacre is told in English and Chinese on it. But it does not mention the massacre of Filipinos.

According to the said books, the massacre of residents in the name of "guerrilla subjugation" were conducted by the X Collective Battalion, composed mainly of the X Infantry Regiment in Los Baños and by the X Amphibious Base Battalion in Bai and San Pablo.

The memorial in the Chinese cemetery, sign says in English, "600 Chinese were massacred by the Japanese Army on February 24, 1945."

Main Street in San Pablo, Laguna. On 24 February 1945, 600 suspected Chinese-Filipinos were killed by the Japanese Imperial Army.

ERASE THE SHADOWS OF PEOPLE IN THE BATTLEFIELD

"Make this area uninhabitable at all"

When I went to the north from Kohriyama Fukushima Prefecture by Shinkansen (bullet train), the color of thickets changed from green into brown. I saw persimmons look like flowers on leafless branches . . . .

I met Bunji Yamazaki at the ticket gate of the station. It's my first meeting with him. He was a small old man, thin like a dead tree. He had sunken eyes.

"My life heavily depended on the outcome of the war. But I was a lucky man. I was recruited in Ranan in Korea, then dispatched to Guadalcanal. We fought fierce battles and many soldiers committed suicide in that island, but I survived because I was a medical officer. I was brought to Japan when I fell sick. My original troop was dispatched to Burma, where another fierce battle was fought. Many soldiers died of starvation there.

Six months later, I was recruited again and dispatched to the Philippines. Because I know how strong the weapons of the U.S. Forces are, I do not want to go to the area in which I had to fight against America. But I had no choice because it was a duty for the country."

He continued with his quiet low voice. "What I can not forget in the war is the subjugation. I did not participate in it directly because I was a medical officer . . . In Los Baños, my comrades threatened Filipinos who took refuge in the church. 'Confess voluntarily if you are guerrillas', they said. And they shot Filipinos if they did not obey them. There were small children, too. But the children just kept silent and stood still. I heard that they set fire on the church after . . . that "

"The local residents claim that as many as one hundred fifty people were burned to death, weren't they? So, the massacre really happened?" I said.

45

His brows were slightly knitted. "I just witnessed a subjugation once. It was in Bai, the town adjoining Los Baños. About thirty Filipinos were brought into a coconut field and killed. Their bodies were then brought to a vacant house to be burned.

Because I was just a soldier, I did not know who ordered that subjugation. But the staff officer of my Army corps was in high spirits. He even ordered, 'Make this area uninhabitable at all.' But the commander of my company said, 'They issued a terrible order.' The village folks courted our favor by bringing us hens and eggs. But they order us to kill those village folks just the same. An order is an order.

But I saw a resident in Bai. When we had gathered the residents, we sneaked into a house because I thought that there would be some food in vacant houses. Though I expected that nobody will be there, I heard something. When I looked inside, I found that an old woman was tremble with fear. Though I repeated 'Running away. Run away.' in Japanese, she could not understand me. So I pushed her. Then she ran away to the back of her house. That is only a consolation for me."

Several days later, I asked him for my interview again over the phone because I wanted to ask some more questions. But he declined. He sent a letter saying that he "lost motivation to meet me again" after reading my previous book.

"It has been forty-six years since then. I felt a pain of reopening our old wounds by the accusation to the soldiers through your book *Walang Hiya*. During that time I belonged to the 16th Base Battalion (the 16th Amphibious Battalion) for my misfortune. But I did not directly kill the residents by myself because I worked as a medical orderly. However, I witnessed the massacres and covered my eyes by seeing the cruel conducts several times. I have never forgotten the miserable situations brought by the war in any single day. I can imagine that the grudge of the Filipino people is still deep-rooted even without reading your report now.

There is no prescription for the crimes to have committed. You did not experience any battle in a foreign land. And I want to ask you how deep you understand the order in the army and the relation between a higher officer and soldiers in which soldiers must obey officers.

It is not permissible that both of the officers and the soldiers became brutal in a frantic state of mind state before the imminent defeat. But even though they demand an apology from us now, many of the soldiers compensated it by their death in the war. Those who survived like me with the devil's own luck desperately contributed for the restoration of our country and helped the reparation of Japan to the other countries. But I do not believe at all that our sin, as a soldier in the troop, already wiped out.

"However, I can not help but lamenting the immaturity of politics, all the more when the victims in occupied countries have yet to be consoled."

We will be called "traitors to Japan" if we criticize that regiment even now

I met Sekichi Fujita in his house. In which he could harvest apples. The fully ripe apple served with tea was tasty. When I had a bite of it, its sweetness spread in my mouth gradually.

After he served as a soldier in Ranan, Korea for three years, he returned to his home and got married. A half year later, he was recruited again and dispatched to the Philippines. He wish that he might not have a child because his newlywed bride would be miserable if he is killed in the war. His father said nothing but his mother said, "Come back alive."

"I can never forget two incidents in the Philippines. The first is the 'guerrilla subjugation' in San Pablo; the second is when guerrillas attacked us in Bai.

I remember the market scene in San Pablo. Noisy tricycles crowded in narrow streets that were lined with many stores owned by the Chinese.

"Because I worked for a signal unit, I did not kill them directly by myself . . . The subjugation was conducted a little bit north of San Pablo, where there was a small pond. There was a small pond. After we forced the residents to dig up trenches to fight against tanks of the U.S. Army, we killed 600 Chinese.

I have been to the Philippines about eight times for the commemoration, but I did not dare go to San

Pablo. But through the introduction by Japanese, who had a good relation with Filipinos, I came to associate with the residents. I also paid tribute to the memorial in the Chinese cemetery which commemorates the massacre of six hundred Chinese."

"I think that the subjugation order was given by the headquarters of the 14th Area Army. I remember its telegraphic message: 'Erase the shadows of the people in the battlefield.' It was called 'Operation Mujinka' (Not-a-single-person-in-sight Operation) at the time."

Later, he sent me a letter describing the nature of the Batangueños, which would explain why we conducted this operation in their province. With his prefatory remark, "I am not in favor of that operation (guerrilla subjugation)," he explained why the captain of X Army Corps ordered it, thus:

> *"Filipinos strongly believe that Batangueños fought in the resistance movement more fiercely than any other ethnic groups. Batangueños traditionally are oppositionists in Philippine politics. I think Jose Rizal, who is from southern Luzon, is a good example.*

"We experienced frequently the fact that those people with such a nature fought a guerrilla war against the Japanese Imperial Army in various areas and they resisted our rule in various aspects before we entered the battle against U.S. Forces. For example, they throw human waste in our kitchen and they steal the vegetables that we bought. They resist in various ways against us. There's the case, for instance of a barrio captain who was a spy.

"Many of my friends fought in the battle in northern Luzon. They said that they had not experienced such conflicts with the people (guerrilla resistance). I think that those factors piled up; that's why the commander decided to issue the subjugation order."

I will return to his testimony later.

"The second incident in the Philippines which I could not forget is when guerrillas attack us in Bai. We slept out in the open on the way from San Pablo to Los Baños after we started on March 2. We were encircled by the guerrillas by midnight. The medical orderlies sleeping beside me were beaten to death. When I was awakened by their screams, I saw that they are already dead. Two soldiers were killed and five were injured. We failed to protect ourselves because we were attacked by surprise.

Our surgeon was missing. He was originally a gynecologist. We searched for him when we did not see his body among the dead. We found him, shuddering at the back of a house; he was all curled up."

"You said that you have been to the Philippines many times. For whom do you hold your memorial service?

"Of course, my comrades. About the commemoration for Filipinos? . . . I have not thought about it.

"May you be allowed to neglect your duty to your comrades and instead give a memorial service for the Filipinos, since their land was made a battlefield and they were killed?" I asked. "Come to think of it, you are right," he said.

I have an episode to tell you. I went to the Philippines because I heard that some amphibious battalion erected a memorial. But what I could find was a mere foundation stone and the rest of the memorial completely disappeared. When I asked about the circumstances, I came to know that the memorial was thrown away the day after the erection. They should not have built it without the consent of the local residents.

Surprisingly, some Japanese cling on past practices. I happened to meet a group of veterans in a hotel when I went to the Philippines for a memorial service. I know, I over heard their conversation during dinner and was astonished to know that they talked as if they are still in the military service. The hierarchy of the army was still practiced or observed. So, they call "Sir, Sergeant" or "Sir, Lieutenant" among themselves. I was pretty astonished.

I am surprised to know that we would be called as "a traitor to the country" if we criticize that regiment even now."

We must not conduct a "subjugation"

I met Yutaro Murakami in a hotel lobby.

"I studied in a seminary because I wished to be a pastor, but I was recruited only four months before my graduation. It was perhaps even before the declaration of war on December 8. I was assigned to the propaganda section of the news division.

I came to San Pablo six months before the corps commander issued a 'subjugation order.' On that order, we disputed thorough because our opinions confronted each other. Ohiwa-san, the commander of the military police in San Pablo, and I insist that we must not conduct a 'guerrilla subjugation.' We argued that it would be impossible to rule the residents after we had engaged the U.S. Forces if we killed the residents. But the commander of the Base Battalion decided the execution in spite of our refutations.

Because we could not say yes to discuss the operation, Ohiwa-san and I discuss and decided to run away before the subjugation. You might think that a captain of the military police was a stubborn military personnel. But Ohiwa-san was not a common military personnel soldier; Filipinos trusted him. He had several friends among them.

In the first place, the propaganda work was in the Philippines. It was substantially wrong to try to achieve the trust from Filipinos even though we occupied a foreign country by our military forces. Because of this reason, the policy of military force and my duty contradict each other. So I pretended to have no knowledge even when I thought that some of the influential figure in the town were fighting as guerrillas. When I knew that the military police were going to arrest one of them, I told them secretly for him to escape. I believed even then that my action was the justice for Japan.

On the day before 'guerrilla subjugation', Ohiwa-san came to me and said that he would run away with the families of the police chief and the mayor of San Pablo. And he asked me to stay behind, though we planned to escape together.

On the day of the massacre, the Japanese Army herded Chinese and Filipinos in the church. I was requested to interpret in English, but I declined the request saying that English could be understood only by some of the residents and that they should ask the interpretation in Tagalog.

The trench digging work was assigned to the Chinese for that day, and Filipino was assigned for the work in the other day. They went home jubilantly. But when the Filipinos went out from the church by fifty persons at a time, Makapili, the Japanese collaborators, checked them up one by one. Makapili selected out about seventy Filipinos on suspicion of being guerrillas. Because one of my assistants was among them, I hurriedly worked for his release. As a result, all the Chinese and about seventy Filipinos who were herded there were executed beside the trench dug up by themselves."

"For no particular reason, I was tried as a war criminal. I became a POW after the defeat of Japan. Because I did nothing wrong, I wrote my real name, my military unit and the place of honestly. In San Pablo, many Chinese were killed as I told. And the Amphibious Battalion burned down a part of the town after in March. Actually the bombing by the Americans destroyed most part of the town.

Soon the investigation on the war criminals started. One day, they brought a list of POWs and said to me: "Point out the soldiers who engaged in the operation in San Pablo." But I found no one who worked in San Pablo. It was because many of the soldiers wrote false names on it when they were captured as POWs as they were afraid of being convicted as war criminals. For example, they used Kiyomasa Kato, Gotoh Matabei, and the names of the other Japanese historical personalities. They used those names to summon Japanese POW. It was funny. This is why I found no familiar names in the list", he said trying to suppress a laugh.

"For this reason, I was convicted as a war criminal as I wrote my name and military unit honestly. The battalion commander committed suicide in the prison camp. He boasted before he was captured: 'I will assume all responsibility for the subjugation in San Pablo.' I suppose that he feared the trial. The company commander, on the other hand, was killed in a battle. As a result, the responsibility for the subjugation in San Pablo was placed on me, the rank and file soldiers. It's injustice, isn't it? In those, times Filipinos so hated the Japanese, they did not care who becomes a war criminal as long as he is Japanese. But when I think about the 600 Chinese and many Filipinos killed there, I can understand their anger. Even though I did not kill their compatriots, my fellow Japanese killed those innocent people."

"Was the subjugation in San Pablo inevitable?" I asked. The situation was not so imminent to conduct it. Because they were losing in the war, they have lost their minds, I think the officers in the corps headquarters were obsessed that they will lose the war and will be killed unless they kill the guerrillas. They pressured us terribly. "Execute the subjugation now," they said.

"Do you want to know if they investigated first whether the residents were guerrillas or not before they were killed? I heard that they were not investigated. This may be the reason why the Chinese have not forgiven us."

"I went to the Philippines several times after the war. I have a Filipino friend in San Pablo. She is already old. Her husband was arrested and killed by the Kempetai. She does not hate the Japanese anymore, she said, because it happened in the past. But she still seems anxious to know where and how her husband was killed and where his body was buried. She tries to convince herself that her husband is dead but fails to understand the fact. It's a natural reaction."

"What do you think of the bill, "UN Cooperation Act", that the Japanese politicians discussed in the Japanese Diet, proposing the dispatch of the Self-Defense Force overseas?"

"Only those politicians with big stomachs can advocate that, because they have not known any actual battlefield," he said cynically.

Let's go there together

When I was preparing for another research in Laguna and Batangas in southern Luzon, a man called me up from western Japan.

"I read your book titled *Walang Hiya*. I want you to correct some of its contents because they are wrong."

He was Yasuo Mizuta. He was assigned at the headquarters of the X Infantry Regiment. He introduced himself in a tone as if he wanted to overpower me.

"Can't you understand what I said? All of the claims by the residents of Bai are all nonsense. I suppose that they just learned of what happened in Calamba and Lipa. And they claim as if they were massacred in Bai. Because their testimony is nonsense, you should correct the contents of your book.

Because I could use English somewhat, I accompanied the corps as an interpreter. That's why I know that their claim about the massacre in Bai is a lie."

"Do you mean to say there was no 'guerrilla subjugation' in Bai?"

"We conducted a subjugation. But we just gathered the residents in the church and checked if they were guerrillas or not. I myself acted as interpreter. We conducted it because the guerrilla was an enemy of the Japanese Imperial Army. We would be killed unless we subjugated them. But we did not kill anyone during that time.

For example, you wrote that six hundred Chinese had been killed in San Pablo. But that's nonsense.

Anyway, the residents were wounded somewhere and just claimed that they were attacked in Bai. But because their testimony is a complete lie, you should write it correctly."

"Though you claim one-sidedly that the testimonies of the residents are nonsense, I can not decide unless I ask the witnesses in the Philippines about it. I will go to the Philippines four days from now. I will visit Bai, too. Do you want to go with me to talk with the residents?

"No, I will never go to Bai."

"Why not? Have you gone to Bai after the war?"

"I have, but I just passed by secretly."

"If so, will you go to Bai again? If you go there, we can clarify the truth."

"I will not go there. It happened forty years ago and we will have only an endless dispute. And I cannot talk on it seriously."

His tone suddenly changed into nervous.

"I understand what you want to say. Because there are still some survivors in Bai who were wounded in the war, I will tell them what you told me so I may know the truth."

"Please do not say that a Japanese claimed it" he said.

"Even though I will not reveal your name to them, I cannot verify the truth without saying that this is the opinion of a survivor among Japanese soldiers, can I?"

"You are correct, but . . .", he said in powerless faint voice.

IT WAS HELL

Raped and killed

I stayed in a hotel by Laguna de Bay in Los Baños. Because the hotel had water supply from a hot spring, I could take a shower of warm water. But the electricity was cut off during suppertime almost every night.

The house of Miss Janesha Derona was located in the outskirts of the town. But I failed to find it and passed it by. When I went back by foot, she walked slowly with her bear feet to her house from the other side of the road as if she could not manage her excessively fat body. About ten red onions with hang in her fat and round hand.

I listened to her experience at the entrance of her small house.

"You said that the Japanese tried to kill every body because they could not identify guerrillas. I cannot agree with it. Because the guerrillas did not live here, but they lived on the mountain. They just came down time to time. But because the Japanese killed even children and women, I will never forgive them."

"Did they say that they had killed the children because the children had helped the guerrillas, too? It is not true. I, myself, and my sisters and brothers had no relation with the guerrilla, though Japanese wounded me and killed my brothers and sisters. Because children could not live on the mountain, they could not contact with the guerrillas. We lived peacefully because we lived at the outskirts of the town. But they suddenly attacked us and started killing us. Do they really believe that they can convince us with such an explanation, even though our family were killed and wounded?

Japanese soldiers were arrogant like a general and they plundered rice, potatoes, vegetable and livestock by force to eat. One of my friends was raped and killed. Because beautiful girls might be raped, I put charcoal on my face to look ugly."

"Do they say that they want to apologize even though they killed my family and wounded me? It is very selfish. I do not want to see them because I hate them. Why they say like that now even though they hurt us tremendously.

I am sorry for you but I hate Japanese very much. They killed my parents and my brothers and sisters. It was six out of my family members. And they even massacred my grandfather and uncles on my mother's side. And I became alone because of the massacre."

"Any message to the Japanese? The Japanese who killed those people devils. I have experienced nothing good since my family was killed. I am still angry and hate them. Although they claim the reasons why they had to kill us, do they really care for those who were killed?"

During a casual conversation with her, I asked about her work. She managed to live by washing clothes of her neighbors and UPLB students (University of the Philippines, at Los Baños).

I hope we will respect each other

The house of Mrs. Segunda Lara, a widow, had been among coconut fields and beyond a small vacant lot from the road before. But the former vacant lot was filled with houses and I could not know how I could reach her house.

She welcomed me with a smiling face. She wore no make-up.

When I handed her monochrome pictures of her taken two years before and compared it with her, I found that she pretty grew old. Several incidents have happened in her family during these two years. Her eldest son has divorced and lived with her with his children. He was three-month-old fetus when Japanese soldier stabbed her with bayonet. When I asked her the reason why he divorced, she simply said that it had been a "family trouble". A girl around two years old sat beside her.

"The claims of the Japanese are strange. They seem to think that it had a matter of course that they must kill guerrillas. But it was the Japanese Army that invaded the Philippines, wasn't it? Japanese army invaded with weapons to the Philippines. And when they committed whatever they wanted, even Filipinos lost patience, didn't they?"

"About my husband. He just protected his family and me and did not side with the guerrillas or with Japanese. To participate in guerrilla activities risked your life then. If they found out a guerrilla, they killed even his family instantly. But many Filipinos became guerrillas in spite of this danger. Risking their lives . . ."

"Are there the Japanese who want to apologize? It is good but . . . I hope that they reveal clearly what they did during the war after they apologize. I hope that they must not deceive on what they did in the past.

And if they are those Japanese who are arrogant and swaggering like before, I do not want to meet them. I will welcome them if they are gentle unlike before. If I revenge on them even though they come here to apologize, my family may be revenged, too. And the killing continues. I believe that I must forgive them because I love peace more than anything else.

It seems that the character of the Japanese is changing recently. One of my daughters is working at the International Rice Research Institute in Los Baños. She is a staff member for a Japanese. She said he is a very nice person. I hope that we can respect each other between Filipino and Japanese from now on."

My small brothers were killed in front of me

The bells on a Catholic church rang in evening gloom and the voice of a priest was heard through a loud speaker.

Miss Fely Olerio was still in the church because she was a devout worshipper. I waited for her for a while in a dark place in the front of her lodging house.

Her room looked like on semibasement floor. And I had to go down by two steps from the front doorstep. It was a simple room. But it was organized tidy. Artificial flowers were on the table.

When I started telling her on the purpose of my visit, she got a word because she could not wait.

"Are those Japanese still alive? Are they still healthy? And what are they saying?"

"They seem to hate and avoid talking on their experience in the war. They keep it as a secret. And they did not reveal it even to their wives. It is hard for them to talk."

"I see. It is because they committed many cruelties in the Philippines. Because they killed indiscriminately even children and babies, they cannot talk on it if they are normal persons. And if they talk on it carelessly, their families must think that they were war criminals and blame them. But if they just keep silence, people will not know what the Japanese Imperial Army did here. I want to ask you again. Is it really true that the

Japanese barely know what the Army did? Even though they committed such cruelties in various places. Is it unimportant incident for the Japanese that those innocent people were killed and died in cold blood in front of them?"

"And do they claim that they killed us to wipe away the guerrillas? I do not want to listen to such an excuse. They killed my mother and my brothers in the front of me and stabbed me down with bayonet. I managed to survive because my mother covered me. But I barely survived in the sea of blood. It was hell."

"Do the Japanese ask our pardon? The former guerrillas might accept their apology, but I doubt if the ordinary residents accept it. I could not forgive them easily.

After the war, I swore to God that I would forgive what the Japanese Imperial Army did because I was a Catholic, but I can never forget the image of my brothers who were killed in front of me. But I will accept those Japanese who wished to apologize if they come here."

"Are you afraid if I will be able to endure even though I am still angry? I have to suppress my angry feeling. It is inevitable that my reason and my feeling will separate away from each other.

Even for a Catholic, it is difficult to forgive them completely. I will never forget the incident because my younger brother was killed in cold blood just in front of me.

So, I do not want to see the Japanese who killed my brother, even when he comes here to apologize. I think it is better not to meet him. Because if I meet him, I may go crazy by recalling the cruel incident in the past," she said with shaking her head slightly.

My grandfathers, mother, and five sisters were not guerrillas

As I went along the road along the shore of Laguna de Bay, I came to see an oval pond with pale blue water on the left side of me. Children were playing in the pond cheerfully. It might be the last place to play in water for them after they could not play in Laguna de Bay because of it is polluted.

I walked down a long familiar path toward the shore of Laguna de Bay. Pedro Orbeta was resting in the house of his daughter, not in the terrace of his own house. It was to avoid strong sunlight.

"Among my family, my grandfathers, my mother and five sisters were killed. It was eight members in total. All of them were not guerrillas. I was not a guerrilla, too. But I had sympathy for Filipino guerrillas. It was because they fought against the Japanese Imperial Army for Filipinos."

In the beginning, his voice lacked energy. But gradually it gained power.

"Did they check whether the captives were guerrillas or not before they started to kill them?" I asked.

"No, they didn't at all. There was a member of the Makapili in this village who collaborated to the Japanese Imperial Army then, but even he was killed indiscriminately. Far from investigating, they attacked suddenly and started killing. They planned to kill everybody. Please think about it. They were cruel soldiers because they tried to kill all the innocent residents. Perhaps their senior officer ordered them. But why such a cruel order was issued even during the war? It was a terrible army."

"The responsibility for the massacre should be shouldered by the one who gave order. If the senior officer did not issue the order, such a massacre did not happened. But even though the soldiers were ordered to do so, they were responsible, too, because they stubbed the residents with bayonet. They killed the unarmed Filipinos who could not resist. If they were human, they should have stopped. But they tried to kill us all. Perhaps they trented us as if we were insects or they looked down on us."

"I have many complains to say to the Japanese. I want them to know the feeling of Filipinos who were killed even though they were innocent. When I remember the incident, anger burns in my heart. It has burned violently for about twenty years, but it has settled down somewhat now. But I could not forget the day when eight members of my family were killed."

Mr. Orbeta's daughter stared at Laguna de Bay from a place under a tree while holding a cup of coffee in her hand. She listened intently to our interview. I asked her opinion.

"I am not complaining to the Japanese. But when I imagine that I had been married to someone and have a child, then the child is killed without reason, it must be painful.

"I understand that the soldiers must obey the order by their senior officers, but I wonder how about the feeling of individual soldiers. When they were forced to kill innocent children, why didn't they express their opinion? It must be difficult, but the soldier could decide if he killed the child standing in front of him because his senior officer did not look on him. I cannot understand why he could not act as an individual person right before killing a baby. He must have complicated feeling, but he must have a good way to avoid killing even babies and children. I could not help feeling that it is only an excuse that they claim they had to kill because they had to obey an order."

A MATTER OF MORALITY

I went to the town center of Bai by jeepney. When I reached the house of Attorney Gitayan, he was on verandah of his house and had his nails taken care of. A young woman beautician cleaned his hands and feet and put transparent manicure on his nails. "You are a rich man." I said unintentionally. But it is a common custom for the middle-class people in the Philippines. "My wife likes it, so I like it, too. But it is cheaper than going to a beauty saloon." He said as if he was apologizing.

His father and elder brother were victimized in the resident massacre by the Japanese Imperial Army. His father was shot dead and his brother became mentally ill. When I visited him on a previous occasion, he said I might meet him if his condition was good. I asked about his brother's condition.

"He is not in a good condition. He is bedridden especially because of this heat. You may visit him next time," he said with knitted brows.

"In Japan, they say, "Might is right." It means that those who won the war are justified and that those who were defeated are treated as wrong in any aspect. If Japanese won against the Philippines and the U.S. in that war, foreigners might not criticize them. But because they were defeated, Filipinos criticize the Japanese and Japanese Imperial Army. This kind of belief still remains in Japan. What do you think of it?

"I do not agree with it. The Japanese left cruel and serious traumas to Filipinos. It is not a matter of win or defeat, but a matter of morality," he said. His darkish face turned reddish-black.

"The Japanese officers and soldiers claimed they were completely ignorant of the Geneva Convention, the rules on the treatment of captives which must be observed during a war?" I said. Though they were ignorant about it, if they still justify their conducts even though they committed grave mistakes, like ordering to kill innocent residents and killing even babies, to comply with the order, they have been wrong up to now from the time during the war," he said.

"I cannot understand why they continue making excuses, not regretting. They must admit their mistake, not continuing poor excuses.

"I have already forgiven what the Japanese Imperial Army did to us long time ago. Because it happened during the war, I even forgave them for the fact that my father had been killed and my brother had been mentally unbalanced. So, I want those Japanese to think over what they did during that time."

Those Insensitive and Shameless Japanese

I went to Victorino Dinero's house whom I met in 1990. But since I forgot the way to his house, I asked a woman in the vicinity and she guided me.

"Do you remember me?" I asked. When he recognized me tension faded away from his narrow brown face. His elder brother whom I am supposed to meet today had died of lung disease the previous year.

"At first, I would like to ask you to recall the day of the massacre on February 9, 1945. On that day, were you brought to a church or a rice mill by the Japanese Army?" I asked.

I recalled the voice of Mizuta-san who had protested to me over the phone saying that the testimonies on the massacre of residents in Bai was a hoax.

"It was a rice mill, not a church. Perhaps it was 1943 or 1944 – I could not remember clearly –when the

Japanese Imperial Army gathered the residents in a church. I did not go there because I was still a boy. But I heard that there was no torturing.

But in the rice mill, they started killing without any interrogation. I was stubbed twice by bayonet. See, there are the wounds here and there," he pointed at his left shoulder and his abdomen.

"A former interpreter for the Japanese Imperial Army protested to me claiming that there had been no resident massacre in Bai and that the so-called war victims in Bai were testifying nonsense. What do you think of his complaint?"

Towards the end of February 1945, Japanese Imperial Army set fire on the town of Lipa. They later escaped and hid in Mt. Malipuyo

"The Japanese guy is a big liar. He confuses the incident in the church and that in the rice mill. I testified what had happened in the rice mill in a war tribunal held by U.S. Forces with showing this scars. That's why an American officer had to take pictures of my scars."

"The massacre was conducted in the rice mill, wasn't it?"

"No, I was not attacked in the mill. Because the inside of the rice mill was so crowded, I was brought to a house in the neighborhood and had my hands tied to a post under the elevated floor behind my back. Then I was stubbed by bayonet.

"Was there a Japanese interpreter?"

"None. They needed no interpreter because they just gathered the residents to kill them."

At first, we were gathered in the rice mill and surrounded by about forty Japanese soldiers. An officer pulled out his *samurai* (Japanese sword). It shone in the morning light. He said something in Japanese. When he swung down the sword, the massacre started. We were brought to the other house to be killed. I was a witness."

"Do you have anything to say to the Japanese who claims that there was no massacre in Bai and that the testimonies by Filipinos are nonsense?" I asked.

"The guy is confusing two incidents. It is a terrible lie to claim that there was no massacre on February 9. They set fire on the town after the killings. If he insists that we are telling a lie, I want him to come here in Bai to talk with us. There are witnesses."

"Some of Japanese think that the soldiers were not responsible because they just obeyed the order from their seniors even though they killed the residents," I said.

"Even though it has been long time since the end of the war, are they still cheating us by saying that they just followed the order? My mother and my brothers were killed even though they were innocent. How do the souls of the victims feel if they know what the Japanese is claiming while the Japanese killed them?

When I think on those shameless Japanese who believe that they need not apologize even though they killed innocent people, my heart aches while recalling the incidents in the past.

Even now when I am talking with you in this interview, I am feeling bitter. If the Japanese are so insensitive, I will never forgive the crimes committed by the Japanese Imperial Army. Please tell them I am still very angry.

A Japanese Sergeant Saved Me

I visited Mr. Gregorio by the introduction of his elder brother who had served as a puppet mayor during the Japanese Occupation. I listened to him while tricycles passed by in the front of us with roar.

"I was one of those residents who were gathered in the church by the Japanese Imperial Army. I am not sure when it had happened, but it was a totally different from the incident happened in the rice mill. Then I worked in the rice mill to polish rice for Japanese Imperial Army. During that time, the Japanese Imperial

Army brought Filipinos to the church to investigate if they were guerrillas. But they did not torture them in that incident. They just slapped those whom they suspected as guerrillas. I think the purpose of this investigation was to arrest guerrillas."

"Was there a Japanese interpreter?" I asked.

"Yes, there was. Though I do not know his name."

"In early morning we were summoned by the Japanese Imperial Army and confined in the church for a week. My wife brought food to me. I remember that I was released after a week and that the guerrilla suspects were also freed the following day.

"All of those gathered there were men. All the men above fifteen years of age in the town were brought there. Because the church was filled with us, there must be more than two hundred people.

"I was saved by a Japanese sergeant. Though I worked in the rice mill, he advised me that I must not stay there and go somewhere else. I was not massacred because of his advice, I thank God."

Malunggay Leaves

I wondered whether I visit there before going back to the hotel in Los Baños. But I stood in front of the house of dentist Amparo Banzon in the end. In my previous interview with her, she criticized me severely because I also served during the war. She angrily said that she would never forgive the Japanese. It was because I had also served the Japanese Army.

In this visit, her face was set in a sulky look same as my previous visit and she coldly allowed me to enter the eight floor of her house.

She sat on a plain chair and extended her hand to a round sallow basket set in the front of her. She started shredding malunggay leaves, from a twig. Perhaps she would put them in a soup.

"The Japanese Army did anything during the war. They did forcibly anything they had planned. But Filipino could not stop their oppression. If they claim that they killed Filipinos because all of the residents were guerrillas, their reasoning is terrible even though they did anything as their pleases."

"Do they say that they had to obey absolutely the order by their senior officers and that they have no responsibility on the massacre for this reason? Then, who will assume the responsibility on the killing of the family of my elder brother? While they claim that they have no responsibility even though they set fire on the church and killed one hundred fifty people, it will be meaningless for me to complain anything.

We were very sad. All of seven members of the family of my elder brother were killed, our house was burned down, and we lost everything. But still they claim that nobody must assume the responsibility for it."

"I have nothing to say to the Japanese. Christianity teach us not to kill others, but it's no use saying to Japanese while they just followed the order to kill and do not regret on what they did even now. I do not want to say anything to those who do not feel their own responsibility. I am very sorry and disappointed."

"Do you have any message for those young Japanese who have not experienced the war?" I asked.

"Rather, I want to say to the Japanese women. Because it is always men who start war in any country, I want Japanese women to watch the activities by men. And though Japan seems to be spending much money for military buildup, they should use the money to help the people in poor countries, because arms are useless. We want to live in peace.

She stopped picking malunggay leaves, I noticed.

Luciano Alcantara: Still Angry After All Those Years

I went to San Pablo. When the bus entered the main street, I saw the shining silver rounded dome of a Catholic church in front of me.

Luciano Alcantara looked far younger than his age, perhaps because he had a full head of black hair. Though it was the first time for us to meet each other, he easily told me his experience during the war when he was fourteen years old. The Japanese Army killed his mother, elder brother, younger sister, and two nephews when they evacuated with him.

"It happened when we were evacuating to Calauan, Laguna. Without knowing that a small troop of the Japanese Imperial Army was stationed there, guerrillas passed by there. The Japanese Imperial Army immediately followed the guerrillas and came to our evacuation site. The Japanese Imperial Army gathered the residents and interrogated them to know the whereabouts of the guerrillas. But nobody could answer. The guerrillas just passed by there to run away; no one knew where they went. Then, the Japanese Army got angry and started killing the residents. I ran away desperately, but five members of my family, including my mother, were killed though they committed nothing wrong.

My father was not killed because he was in a different place. I was very sorry and cried frequently because I was just a boy."

"Do you have any message for the Japanese?" I inquired.

"Of course, I have. Please tell them that I have not forgotten the incident and I have been angry all these forty-six years. You will understand why I am still angry if a foreign army invaded Japan and its soldiers killed your parents, brothers, and sisters for no reason.

I cannot understand. The Japanese seem to think that it was not wrong for them to kill the innocent residents and that the guerrillas must be blamed for it. I hope they recall the past honestly in front of God.

My father was a guerrilla and he was killed

Mrs. Lita Pontanosa was a short and thin woman.

"My father was killed when I was thirteen years old."

Perhaps it was first time for her to meet a Japanese since the end of the war, she became tense and started talking in soft voice.

"It was when we evacuated from San Pablo to a barangay. During lunchtime, Japanese soldiers and Makapili came to our house and they said to my father that there would be a gathering in an elementary school and that he must attend it in the afternoon. But my father did not go to the school but to our field. As he met with my aunt on the way to the field and she blamed him for he would not go to the school, he changed his mind and went to the school. When he and other residents entered the school, everybody was tied on their hand behind their backs. And three persons among them were brought to a barrack as suspects of guerrilla activity. My father was among them. He was confined there for about six months. Though we brought food for him everyday, it seemed that he could not receive it, because the Japanese soldiers ate it.

Then, two men were released, but my father was kept there. I heard that he was killed in a night. But we do not know on the details. We even do not know where my father was buried.

Though my father was a member of the guerrilla, he was a very kind and good man. If the Japanese Imperial Army had not come, he would not have become a guerrilla and would not have been killed."

"It was very hard for us since my father was killed. I did anything to help my mother. I went to the town to sell vegetables and brought goods in the market to sell in the barangay. I helped in harvest of rice to receive unhulled rice. I washed clothes of rich families. I did everything to earn money."

"I still hate the Makapili. Because they sold my father to the Japanese even though they were same Filipinos, I can never forgive them. But I heard that it was Japanese, not a Makapili, who killed my father.

But I am not angry at the Japanese anymore. Since ten years after the Liberation, I came to forgive them gradually. But I will never forget what happened to us."

Both Filipino and Japanese Love Their Families

I have met Azucena Ocampo several times in Japan and the Philippines. Her house was located in Los Baños and it was near the hotel where I am staying, but I met with her in the playing garden with a hot spring she manages with her husband.

Eight persons from her family were killed, leaving only her, when she was six years old. She was called Susie then. Those who were killed are her parents, her grandmother, her younger brother and younger sister, her aunt, and an unborn child because her mother was pregnant. She was stabbed four times by bayonet but she managed to survive.

"Though the Japanese Imperial Army claimed that even women and children worked for guerrillas, I was not a guerrilla or a collaborator. But I was almost killed. Perhaps some of adults were collaborators but the children would not know it. My younger brother and younger sister were killed without knowing anything.

By the way, when I attended a gathering in Kyoto, a former Japanese soldier came there to apologize. He said 'If I did not kill you as I was ordered, I might be killed or excluded from our group for the charge that I violated the order by the senior officer.' And he also said, 'The society would discriminated not only me but also my family. So it was inevitable for us to stab you.' He said with tear in his eyes. But I was not feeling fine when I think on my family who were killed."

She told me on her experience during her visit to Japan, by the invitation by the Forum to Reflect upon the War Victims in the Asia-Pacific Region and Engrave It in Our Minds. In this visit, she had told her experiences during the war to her Japanese audience.

"The Japanese Imperial Army killed Filipinos without hesitation. One of my relatives was raped then killed. My great-grandfather was a landowner in this area but he was interrogated together with his servants to check if they were guerrillas. Then he was tied to a column of his house with barbed wire. And they set fire on his body. Though he shouted for help, the people had to hide around the house and could not do anything to help him because the Japanese soldiers still stayed there."

"I still remember that the Japanese Imperial Army used the ground floor of our house as the headquarters of the troop and the church on the next door as the barracks. During that time, Japanese soldiers were not so violent. They taught Japanese language in the school and played with us. I remember that we were very happy.

But after U.S. Forces landed on Luzon Island and their bombing became strong, Japanese army became cruel. My uncle on my father said that U.S. Forces recovered 2000 captured soldiers from the prison camp placed in UP campus in the end of February of 1945. The Japanese Imperial Army fled to mountain by that attack, but Filipinos cheerfully welcomed Americans. By this act, the Japanese got irritated, felt jealous and started killing the residents around Anos when Americans went away."

"You said that some Japanese want to apologize on what they did during the war. It is very good. Because I believe in God, I think it is very good if the Japanese apologize and we can reconcile each other."

"I will tell you about the experience of a former Japanese soldier. I met with him in Japan. He was ordered to kill the residents including women and children in Batangas. While his senior officer went away for a while, he shot his gun to the sky and said to the residents, 'Run away now.' But the resident could not move because they were so terrified. How many times he said them to run away, they could not understand because he did not know Tagalog language. After a while, his senior came back and he had to kill them. Even though an individual soldiers wanted to help, sometimes he could not do it in a war or in an army organization."

"At first, I hated the Japanese. Because I became alone, I continued to be distressed even I thought that I would be rather killed with my family. But while I met several Japanese, I noticed that they are same humans.

"While I thought on why those Japanese had been so cruel, I noticed that the war changed them. I came to think that the war had changed the characteristic of those Japanese.

"Though I forgive the war crime committed by Japanese, I will never forget my miserable experience. So I hate wars and I hate violence. Even the Gulf War and other war in the foreign countries terrify me. It is because even babies and children are killed in a war, just as we experienced.

"While I stayed for about two weeks in Japan, I was surprised to know that Japanese were wonderful people while Japanese had killed all of my family members in the war.

"Before I went to Japan on the invitation of the Forum to Reflect upon the War Victims in the Asia-Pacific Region and Engrave It in Our Minds, my son was worried for my trip. He said, 'You should not go there because the surviving Japanese soldiers might get angry and kill you if you talk on your experience during the war as a Filipino who were wounded by Japanese soldiers.'

"So I met with the town mayor to consult with him on the apprehension of my son. The mayor advised me, "The Japanese are kind and courteous.

And you have nothing to worry about. You should say what you have in your mind. If you are still angry, you should express it clearly. If they intend to hurt you, they might as well not have invited you.' What he said was true.

"When I arrived in Japan, I found that it was a very nice place. If I had money, I wanted to bring my family to Japan. It was clean and beautiful anywhere in Japan and people were kind, too. I had a chance to see a Japanese family when I stayed in the house of a doctor in Niigata. The doctor, his wife, and their children were very kind. I came to know that in this occasion that both Filipinos and Japanese love their family".

CHAPTER 3

LIPA AND
ITS SUBURBS

I listened to the claims of Filipinos on the resident massacres, called as "guerrilla subjugation" by the Japanese Imperial Army, conducted in Panay Island and Laguna, Batangas, Quezon and other provinces in Luzon. I published them in my first book. I was shocked strongly when I found that the Japanese committed massive and cruel resident massacre while I made a research in Lipa City and surroundings in Batangas.

On February 27 and 29, 1945, one month after the corps commander issued the order of "guerrilla subjugation," the male residents from three barrios were gathered in a seminary in Pamintahan near the town. Because the Japanese Imperial Army said that they would give passes to the residents (permissions to move around the area issued by Japanese Imperial Army), the residents went into a coconut field. But they were stabbed with bayonet there and thrown down into a river thirty meters below. According to the estimate by a former Japanese soldier who participated in this operation, about 1,000 people were killed in two days. And based on the claim by the residents, 1,500 to 2,000 people were massacred in this incident.

The Airfield Battalion, the Machine Gun Platoon of the Infantry Regiment, and other corps stationed there and were responsible for this incident.

And even in the barrios around Lipa City, resident massacres were committed in thirteen places as long as I could research. In Barrio Posel and Barangay Pagao, the Japanese Imperial Army brought the residents the side of a deep well and stabbed with bayonet to throw them into the well.

And in a barrio on the foot of Maralaya mountains (Mt. Malipuyo is the main mountain among them), men and women, children and even babies were massacred. Especially the residents of Barrio Lumban and Barrio Solok were brought to the forest in Quemuros and Pulihan in the side of the same river and killed and thrown into the valley. A monument was erected in Lumban with the following message in Filipino on it.

Dapat malaman ng lahat na dito nalibing ang mga kalansay ng mga tao mahigit na isang libo (1,000) bata at matanda pinatay ng mga Hapones noong guierra, Marso 4, 1945 na tagarito sa Barrio Lumbang, Solok at pagitan at napatayo ito, sa pagmamalasakit nina: (March 4, 1945 during the war, Japanese Imperial Army massacred the residents including children and adults in Lumban, Solok and other villages. More than 1,000 dead bodies were buried here. Everybody knows this incident).

DAPAT MALAMAN NG LAHAT NA DITO NA LIBING ANG MGA KALANSAY NG MGA TAO MAHIGIT NA ISANG LIBO (1,000) BATA AT MATANDA PINATAY NG MGA JAPONES NOONG GUIERRA, MARZO 4, 1945 NA TAGARITO SA BO. LUMBANG, SOLOK AT PAGITAN, AT NAPATAYO ITO, SA PAGMAMALASAKIT NINA:

MR. CECILIO AQUINO & FAMILY
MRS. URBANA HOLGADO
MR. MAXIMINO HERERA
MR. LAUREANO HERERA
MR. SALVADOR CRUZ
MR. NICOLAS MAGALING
MR. PEDRO BILOG
MR. BENJAMIN RECENO
MR. ROSENDO HARAVE
AT IBA PA

Tagalog epigraph on the memorial shrine for massacre victims in Lumban, Batangas

The Airfield Battalion of the Japanese Imperial Army, which had a garrison in Lipa, took part in the guerrilla subjugation of the barrios around Lipa.

I WILL BRING THE TRUTH INTO MY GRAVE

I don't feel sorry at all

I rode on a train of private railways going to suburbs and got off at a small station. Fields were seen in-between residential areas here.

When I reached out my hand to the door of the ready-built house facing a road, it opened smoothly. When I called out, Seita Saito appeared with dragging his leg. He wore reading glasses and looked haggard.

He guided me to a room with a Japanese-style stove and stretched his stiff leg under the table. He was strafed by machine gun fire from an American-piloted Grumman fighter plane while he worked for the airfield in Lipa. The bone in his right ankle suffered a compound fracture. As his right leg was cut twice in hospitals in the Philippines and Japan from his knees, he attached an artificial leg on his right leg.

"Because I stayed in Lipa for six months before I was wounded, I participated in subjugation time to time. When Makapili gave us an information, we attacked guerrillas while they were sleeping. So we did not have much work during daytime. We sometimes played with children.

When we captured a suspected Filipino guerrilla, we tied his hands behind his back. And we hung him down with string and tortured him to investigate.

One night I went to a farmland owned by a Japanese in Ibaan. I heard a familiar Japanese song. It went . . . like this: 'With saying nothing, in Yasukuni Shrine . . .' The Japanese were growing cotton with local workers. Four Japanese asked me saying, 'We want to participate in a guerrilla subjugation.' When I asked the reason, one of the Filipinos answered to me before the Japanese. He said that Filipino men had approached to a Japanese soldier with saying 'Tomodachi, cigarette please' and they shot the soldier suddenly with a gun which they hid. So they wanted to revenge.'

The following day, we went out for subjugation and captured men. And we brought them to the farmland in Iban to torture. One of them said that he was a schoolteacher and that he was cooperating for Japanese Imperial Army by teaching Japanese language. Because he did not confess, we repeatedly punched him while hanging him down from the ceiling. Because he kept silent, our captain pulled his sword out and threatened him saying, 'I will kill you unless you will not confess while I count ten.' As he answered 'I will confess', we brought him down. But he did not answer clearly that he was a guerrilla. So we repeated torturing again and our captain gestured to cut his neck. Then, he finally opened their mouse. But he said defensively 'Though I hate the Japanese Imperial Army in my heart, I have been cooperated with them.' He made another excuse. When we asked him who was the boss, he answered 'he is now travelling'. His answer was very smart. We had a hard time with him.

Of course, we killed those who were tortured so that we would have no trouble later."

"I don't think that we did anything wrong to Filipinos at all. The man has to live in the given time and situation. During that time the guerrilla was our enemy and we were trained to kill the enemy when we found them. It was a common sense then, so I don't think we committed anything wrong. I recall those time even with some affection."

"Do you still think in this way?" I asked.

"Of course, I still do. It was war and we had to kill each other."

"Do you want to know how I think on the war while I lost my leg? We have to live our lives by building up our destiny and by giving up what was lost. And I think it is satisfactory as long as I can live an ordinary life."

Yukichi Yamashiro: Drenched with Blood

I knocked on the door of the room of the third floor of the local government apartment building. And I produced my calling card with starting introducing myself. But he seemed to take me as a high-pressure salesman and he yelled at me abruptly.

"I am busy now. What do you want?" he asked.

When I explained the purpose of my visit, he lowered his voice. "I am about to leave because my wife is in a hospital. But you may enter," he said.

Yukichi Yamashiro was a private first class for maintenance in the Lipa Airfield Battalion.

"When I was in the Philippines, I did what I would never do in our normal life. When we went for patrolling, we killed eight children and women. During that time, we were ordered to kill any Filipino if we saw him. We killed them after tying their hands behind their backs. I killed two of them. I stabbed them with all my might with my bayonet which went through from his chest to his back, I was surprised to feel that their blood was warm. The sergeant killed the rest. I was drenched with blood from my hand to my chest.

Then, we threw all of them into a well. In the following day, when we looked down the well, a middle aged woman was hanging on the grass grew on the wall of the well. She was holding an old woman by her other hand, so that the old woman would not sink in the water. But the sergeant held a stone . . ."

He gestured to hold up a stone with two hands with saying.

"He threw the stone which hit her head. I still see this scene in my nightmares and wake up shivering."

"Do you ask me if I told this experience to my wife? No, I didn't. I did not tell it to anybody. We could not commit such a cruel act normally. But we did it because we were ordered to do so."

"If we recall it, do we have a reason to kill the women and the children while they did not resist us? But we were ordered to kill them..."

"Was it possible for us to make them escape? I doubt the possibility."

He faltered and looked away.

"By the way, we have complaints, too. Even though the soldiers fought at the risk of their lives, they could not receive any decoration. Those who worked in safe places receive medals, while those who fought in the risk of their lives were not rewarded at all. I hope that we are treated more carefully. I could not receive even the pension for veterans because I did not serve for fifteen years. Though I applied twice, I received only 25,000 yen as a lump-sum payment because the period of my service was short by only fifteen days."

He poured hot water into my cup from a pot as if he happened to remember it.

Because his wife had lived in one of the biggest industrial areas in Japan for a long time, she repeated entering hospitals for some sickness with asthma resulted from pollution.

Kenji Oda: Both Sides are to Blamed

When I learned Kenji Oda is working in a machine maintenance shop, I went to see him.

Among the machinery covered with dust and oil, a tall guy in his working clothes showed up. Even though it was already noontime, his clothes were not dirty. He might be a supervisor.

"I heard that you were convicted as a war criminal."

"It was a hoax. As long you are a Japanese, you could be punished."

He stared at me. His face was red, dish and grim. He said it was cold and guided me to a field office; there a gas stove heater was on and I noticed its reddish yellow flame.

"In Lipa, we did it near a mountain stream. I was there. The order came from Yamashita Army Corps. But they told us we must not do it that much. We killed almost all the men in the village."

"Did you stab them with a bayonet and throw them in the river?" I asked.

He stiffened his face, but said nothing.

"Do you feel sorry for those Filipinos?"

"No, I don't. It happened during the war. Both sides are to blame. We were not safe even from women and children. They brought grenades under bananas in a basket and shot us with a pistol. Even women fought against us. I saw it with my own eyes that a woman approached a soldier, used her sexual charm and suddenly she shot him with a pistol, which she hid. We could not be too careless around them."

"Do you know why the Filipinos became guerrillas?" I asked.

"Well, maybe we plundered food from them. Because the Japanese Imperial Army rarely supplied us with goods, we had to commandeer food to eat."

"Do you want to know the incidents which I can't forget . . . Well, it was the guerrilla subjugation. I cannot forget the cries and weeps of women and children before they were thrown into a well. They are still lingering in my ears. We stabbed them once with bayonet and threw them into the well. Because the wells in the Philippines were wide in the bottom, we could throw more than three or 400 people safely. In the last, we threw them without stabbing."

"In the beginning, we could not kill even a man. But we managed to kill him. Then, we hesitated to kill a woman. But we managed to kill her, too. Then, we could kill children. Those soldiers who had children back in Japan said that they could not kill a child. But he also got accustomed to killing children, while he was killing them hesitantly. We came to think as if we were just killing insects. Our feeling has changed as if we were slapping a fly casually with a fly swatter.

We threw down residents in some subjugation. When I went out for patrolling the following day, I saw that a survived woman was combing her hair on dead bodies. I threw a grenade in the well. During that time, the principle of the army was to kill even women, children, and old men.

One day, I saw that an old woman was bringing down some food in a basket for the survivors in the well. Because we had to kill everybody, I killed her, too."

I talked on the possibility of apology for those war victims in the Philippines again.

"Though you talk on it again, I do not feel like apologizing to them. It was done during the war, I did not like to kill them. I was forced to do so by the order. Rather I feel sorry for my subordinates who were killed in the war."

Because he was a sergeant, he had a few subordinates.

"Have you gone to the Philippines for a memorial service of your comrades?"

"No, I haven't. I do not want to go," he said.

"A Filipino from Batangas worked in this factory before and he said that the Japanese Imperial Army killed his father. But I could not tell him that I had been in Lipa during the war."

All the Men in the Village

Motokichi Yamamoto has just finished trimming pine trees. His hands were huge and rough like roots of trees; they were dirty and caked with pine resin.

.I handed him my calling card with introducing myself and said that I wanted to know his war experience when he was in Lipa serving under the Airfield Battalion.

"About Lipa. I do not want to talk about it. I really hate to do so. I experienced various incidents in the war.

I did not do this act but I brought the men to the gathering place after they were summoned in another place."

He gestured the stabbing with bayonet with saying, "I did not do this act."

"My role was to watch over the situation from a hill away from the town of Lipa. It was called 'Lipa Hill' (now called Anilao Hill).

I brought the residents from the gathering place to the site of the massacre in a coconut farm on the day of the incident. It was our duty.

But because those men never come back once we brought them, women and children came to our observation post the following day and they blamed us. It lasted for three days and three nights. They cried, "Bring my husband back!" and "Give my son back!" Because we could not tell the truth that we had killed them, we pretended to know nothing and endured. But we could not bear on the grudge of the woman.

Do you want to know the number of the victims? I am not sure, but I heard that they killed almost all the men in the village.

I feel sorry for those Filipinos because we devastated their land and because we killed them."

"My feeling with recalling my war experience. We must not start a war anymore. I always tell my wife and children that war is cruel. While we watch television news on Gulf war and it looks like fire works, it is only a kind of child play. The real war is tragic."

"Do you ask me if I have talk on the cruel subjugation to my family?" I asked.

"No, I couldn't. This is the first time that I talk of it in front of my wife," he said.

His wife was looking down the kotatsu (under-the-table heater) with her shoulders hunched. She seemed older than him.

"I went to the Philippines once to see the sights. I went around Taal Lake and passed by Lipa where the Airfield Battalion had stationed. I found out that there was still an airfield. Every time I had coconut milk and a warm wind blows, I recall the grudge of the women who cried, "Bring my husband back." Though I tried to forget, their sorrow and resentment comes alive again to me. I don't want to go to the Philippines anymore," he said.

When I was going to leave, he took out a newspaper clipping among his papers. He had kept it a secret to his wife.

"This article covers the details of the Lipa subjugation, although I could not explain it well," he said.

He held an article titled "World and People" on 30 July 1989 in *Mainichi News*. The article carried the picture of Marcelino Magaling and his testimony. His face was familiar to me. All of his family was killed in the massacre when he was seven years old. (I will show the interview with him later in this book.)

"I could returned alive, perhaps because I did not commit wrongdoings a lot," he said from behind me while I put on my shoes.

Tameshigiri or Testing the Samurai

When I got off at the station where the bullet train stops, cold rain was falling. I took a taxi from a subway station to visit Motoyuki Osawa. He appeared at the front door of his house, with a suspicious look on his narrow wrinkled face.

"I was a fresh recruit trained in Manchuria. We were frequently beaten then. The noncommissioned officer assigned to train us slapped us a lot. He said that we would become cowards and run away from our enemies in the front line when bullets were shot against to us, if they will not punch and train us severely.

"After we retreated to Mt. Malipuyo once and when we attacked the town of Lipa, I was wounded on my ear and head severely. I regained consciousness in a hospital of the U.S. Forces. I didn't know how many days I was unconscious. I fell ill of malaria and dengue fever then and I got in a condition as if I was mad. I was treated excellently in the American Army hospital. A lot of meat was served to me; I became fat rapidly.

97

An interpreter for me is of Japanese descent and made arrangements for me to have rice twice a week. He said, "Because you are Japanese, you must like rice." I was also given milk and cakes. An American soldier lies on the bed next to me. Because that Japanese American saved my life, I went to look for him to thank him, when I returned to Japan. But I wasn't able to find him."

"Since we went out for subjugation many times, we had various experiences. When we have captured young men, we put them in a trench. We then try our swords on them, pulling them out one by one. We also tortured them.

Whenever we go to a village, we surround it and set fire on the houses. If we didn't do so, we might be shot. We then shoot to kill everybody once they jump out of their houses.

But the guerrillas were also cruel. One day we entered a big house in some subjugation and opened a closet. A dead body of a Japanese soldier fell down from it. All its fingers were cut. When I saw it, I got mad and made up my mind to kill guerrillas, because I was still young."

"Do you know that the Japanese Imperial Army conducted a "guerrilla subjugation" for two days near a mountain stream in the town of Lipa?" I asked.

"Yes, I know it but . . ."

"Did you participate in it?" I asked.

He lowered his head and nodded slightly.

"What did you do?" I asked.

"My samurai broke in two in that subjugation. I tried to cut a man down with it but it hit his shoulder. I failed."

"Was it *tameshigiri* ('sword testing')?" I asked

"Yes, I did. When the officer did it, the sword was broken into two. It was an important sword for me, because my elder sister bought it for me. I am sorry, but I cannot tell some more. I do not want to recall what happened then."

After the subjugation, I recalled it for two or three days and could not sleep well. I had a fever as if my blood rose up to my head.

This condition is still with me. After I talked on my experience like today, I would not be able to sleep for a few days. I have nightmares when I remember the 'guerrilla subjugation.'

Like Robots

The train was running with making big curve along coastal line. I remembered the words of Toshiyuki Nishizaki. I met him in a hospital the previous day, while on the train I was looking at a calm sea, which appeared from time to time.

*Mt. Malarayat, viewed from the
Catholic church in Lipa*

"Nobody is able to express the truth of the tragedy in Lipa. We must keep it in our heart to bring into our graves. The hearts of any soldiers are filled with such feeling," Nishizaki-san said.

He was one of the participants of the massacre in Pamintahan, Lipa on 27 February 1945. Though I wanted to know his feeling in detail, I had to give up my plan. He must be in complete rest as he had undergone an operation only four days earlier.

Then I got off the last station of Japan Railways. I went to Yoshio Yamamoto's house by taxi from the station of Japan Railways. But he was not at home and was attending the commemoration rite for war victims in a town hall. He was an influential resident of the town.

As he said that he could be free after 12 p.m., I waited for him at the reception room in the splendid town hall for two hours. And I read the program of the commemoration rite.

Opening remark. National anthem. Silent prayer. Poetry reading. Offering of flowers. Acknowledgment from the leader of the bereaved families. Closing remark.

When I read through the program, I found that the "Song of Yasukuni Shrine" and "Song for War Victims" were printed on it.

Yamamoto-san wore a marine blue suit and big white artificial flower on his chest. His long face has deep wrinkles.

"What do you want to know? Do you want to know about the unforgettable experience in the Philippines? Perhaps it will be that I managed to survive by hiding in mountains until I returned to Japan alive.

I also participated in the ordinary fight in the war and attacked the enemy once. But because we were fought back immediately, we ran away at once. The firepower of the enemy was tremendous. It was a war between babies and adults. They set fire on jungles and coconut farms to remove everything. And then they came with tanks at the front. We could do nothing against that strong firepower. The Japanese Imperial Army was defeated one-sidedly.

When I recall now, we were cruel to Filipino residents. We forced guerrillas dig up holes on the ground, and ordered young soldiers to cut down the guerrillas. We claimed that we were training the young soldiers. I also killed one guerrilla. When I stabbed him, he fell down. I could not help but stabbing him to death while he lay on the ground.

It was just what I heard, but other soldiers captured the residents and threw them into a well. Then they killed the residents by throwing down a grenade to them. I heard another inside story in Lipa. The soldiers deceived the residents. They said that they would give certificates. But they brought the residents to a mountain river and killed over it."

He looked up and became silent.

"I am now thinking after running under flying bullets and becoming old to this age. I think that the objective of man is to live an honest life and to have children who succeed him. But many comrades were killed in the war."

"Do you claim that many people were also killed in the Philippines where the land was used as a battlefield?

"Yes, you are right."

"Do you feel sorry for those war victims in the Philippines?" I asked.

"No. an order is an order." he said.

"Do you think that it may be possible to decide by myself while the senior officer was not present, even though I was strictly ordered to kill all the people in the area. No, it was not possible. The battlefield was an abnormal area and we became abnormal, too," he said.

"Those Filipino victims said that the Japanese must have their own decision and responsibility before they stabbed them with bayonets as long as they had not been robots.

"But the soldiers completely behaved like robots during that time."

"In this year, they will hold a comrades' meeting, but I have not attended such a meeting yet. They maintained the same relation as the army among them. Because I was a fresh recruit, I was forced to work as hard as a robot. I do not feel my former comrades as old friends even when I meet them.

I heard that a high-ranking officer keeps a woman companion in a cave on Mt. Malipuyo, even when they were driven into it by the U.S. Forces."

"What I learned from the war is that we must not fight in our country but in a foreign country at least, even when we were forced to fight a war. I always insist on. We can avoid making our land a battlefield.

"I believe that a country must have a certain level of armament. But we do not need tanks for the battle in this country. It is because we are already defeated when we start ground battles in this country. If it is inevitable to fight a war, we must fight out of this country. If not, we will see the miserable situation same as in the Philippines."

"Who is responsible for World War II? General Hideki Tojo led this country to the wrong direction. It was a mistake to enshrine him in the Yasukuni Shrine."

"I went to the Philippines only once after the war. I went there to collect the remains of my comrades, but I could not look at the faces of the old men. I was afraid they would tell me: 'You are the soldier who had come here.'"

"Today, we had a commemoration rite in this town. Commemoration for Filipino victims . . . No, I have not considered it yet," he said in a tone as if he came to think of it only for the first time.

"PLEASE BRING MY HUSBAND BACK"

I want to strangle them

It is said that the Japanese Imperial Army deceived and killed about 400 men from Barrio Lotlot, Calamba, Laguna on the second day of the massacre, same as what happened on the first day.

Andre Laronio was one of those victims who were tricked. But he barely escaped and survived. He was brought to a coconut farm, but he desperately tried to untie a rope that bound him secretly to watching Japanese soldiers. Just when the soldiers came in front of him, splashed with blood of the victims on their bodies, while they were stabbing other Filipinos with bayonets, he succeeded in untying the rope that connected him with the man behind him. Though his hands were still tied together behind his back, he ran away with all his might. When two Japanese soldiers ran after him, he jumped into a mountain stream from a high cliff. When he hit the river's bottom, he only injured his face, and survived.

He holds a party and invites his relatives on February 28 of each year to thank God—for the Japanese Imperial Army wasn't able to kill him.

When I visited him, he was not at home, because he had a medical check up in a hospital in Manila. His son's wife said, "He has an enlarged heart, but we worry about him because he is already old."

Mr. Laronio's wife approached me with uncertain steps. She looked pale and her hair was uncombed. She has more white hair than before.

"They say they tried to kill all the men in Lotlot because all of them were guerrillas?" she stared at me while saying this in a hoarse voice.

"Did they kill the collaborators for guerrillas? As long as we are Filipinos, all of us had sympathy for the guerrilla, except for Makapili. If you think on what Japanese Imperial Army did in the Philippines, it is easy for you understand the reason. But two of my uncles were killed. Though my husband was not killed, he was a victim, too.

So we are still angry. We could not help being angry. Whenever I see the children of my brothers, I get angry at those Japanese who killed their father. I feel like wringing their necks," said.

She stuck her hands with veins stood out on them out to me and gestured to chock a neck up.

"Is it true that some Japanese feel sorry for us? But I don't want to see those Japanese who killed my elder brothers. If I see those Japanese, I will only suffer by recalling the past.

"But if they want to come here to apologize, I want them to compensate the war victims before their visit. My brothers were killed for nothing. While they were in their thirties and forties, in the ages to work hard, their families did not receive anything. If the Japanese pay such compensations, I might accept their apology. I don't think I am greedy. Though they killed 2,000 people in Pamintahan, nobody paid even one peso and apologized for it."

Five Japanese Soldiers and a Pregnant Woman

At first, I have decided I would no longer go to Barangay Anilao. The residents of this barangay could not forgive the Japanese as they killed 700 men. They deceived them and said that they would give them passed. They blamed me twice there, thinking that I am a representative of the Japanese who had served during the war. I took on a jeepney to Anilao. Anyway, I forced myself to go there.

Sergio Garcia stood in his small garden. Though he wrote to me in his letter that it was difficult to go out to his field because of his asthma, he looked not so pale.

He is the only survivor of the Pamintahan massacre. Though he was stabbed five times on his body with a bayonet and two of these stabs even went through his body from his chest to his back, he crawled out from the piled up bloody bodies of victims and managed to survive.

"I want to ask to those surviving Japanese soldiers why they tried to kill me even if I was just a farmer, though they claim that they cut down Filipino because they were guerrillas. I want to know the reason," he started saying, his sunken eyes glaring.

"Do you want to know whether or not the Japanese Imperial Army conducted an investigation in the seminary where we were herded? No, they investigated nothing. They just lied at us saying that they were going to give us passes and brought us out in groups of twenty people at once. I never expected that I would be included in Pamintahan. So we followed them because I believed in what they said . . ."

"You say that their claim was like this, 'We are not responsible for the massacre because we were just ordered, while we had to obey any order absolutely.'

After the massacre in Pamintahan, five Japanese soldiers raped a pregnant woman. Another Japanese raped a woman even when she was eight-months pregnant, after he had killed her husband. Do they claim that they were not responsible for it because they were ordered for it?"

"Is it true that there are some Japanese who want to apologize to the war victims in the Philippines? That's remarkable. If they want to apologize, I will forgive even those Japanese who tried to kill me. But you also said that some of those Japanese believed that they didn't need to apologize even though they killed Filipinos indiscriminately. I wonder what kind of men they are. I can not help thinking that they are only animals.

"But even though I will forgive, many residents in this barangay are still angry. I don't know if they will forgive, too.

But I thank God because I survived."

His wife had much white hair on her head. She started saying, "Because my husband was stabbed in the chest and the bayonet went through to his back, he fell ill of asthma for those wounds. He could not work in the field. I want those Japanese to compensate him. He has to go to hospitals and buy medicine. When I brought him to a doctor, the doctor said that the cause of his asthma is the wounds inflicted by the bayonet."

"I want them to explain why they nearly killed me. I cannot accept their excuse that I was a guerrilla or that they were ordered."

When I was about to leave, I thanked him for the interview. But he strongly persuaded me to have lunch.

On a big hand-made table in the adjacent room, boiled beans, sweetened jackfruit, and newly rice were set. At first, they thought I was hesitating a little with a spoon and fork in my hands.

His wife spoke to me from the kitchen, "Don't be afraid. We didn't put poison in your food."

Toubatsu Meirei or The Subjugation Order

I went to Barangay Pagao in Lipa by tricycle. Two old men were chatting on a small bench in front of Sisenando Tolentino's house. I didn't notice that one of them was Sisenando. His face was heavily wrinkled and his body has shrank a bit. While handing out pictures of him taken two years ago, I wondered why he had aged so rapidly.

"Japanese soldiers attacked this barrio early in the morning. They captured my father, two of my elder brothers, my uncle and me, while we were in our house. They tied us in groups of threes and brought us in front of a deep well near our house. Then they stabbed the victims with bayonets and threw them down the well at once.

We, the younger members of our family, were at the end of the line. We talked among ourselves and made a decision. We will jump into the well before they can stab us. The moment we are about to be stabbed, the three of us jumped together into the well.

109

The Japanese soldiers shot us with their guns all together. One of us was killed, but the others, including me, survived marvelously. God saved us. We had jumped on the dead bodies, not into water. More than sixty people had already been killed when we jumped.

The deep well in Pagao, Lipa, where more than sixty skeletal remains still lie.

"Even though the Japanese killed as many as sixty residents at once, they claim that they killed them because they were guerrillas. How can they claim such an excuse even though they never investigated whether we were guerrillas or not. They stabbed us to death and threw us down the well we were men.

And though more than forty years has passed, they do not apologize nor pay any compensation. Even one peso. Filipinos are keeping silent because we are gentle . . . "

"The Japanese blame the orders though they have committed the massacre. They raped a woman and then killed her. Were they also ordered to rape her? As long as they are human, they must think in their mind before they kill or rape anybody. Blaming the order issued by their senior officer for everything is the height of irresponsibility, I think.

"Is it recent or a long time ago when they said that it was inevitable because they were ordered by the senior," asked.

"I heard of it only recently," I said.

"Is it only recent when you heard such a claim from them? It means they have no regret at all, though they committed such a cruel act."

"But they have not told the reality of the massacre in Lipa to any member of their family, even though they claim that it was inevitable because they were ordered. Is it true that they keep it secret even to their wives? It is because the Japanese know in their heart that they committed a fatal sin. That's why they want to hide the truth even from their families."

I went out the door after I had thanked him for the interview. I looked at the place diagonally opposite of unpaved road without much attention. Under banana leaves, I saw a frame of a deep well covered with moss that was built in Spanish time. More than sixty skeletal remains still lie.

If those Japanese will appear in front of us

Men and jeepneys always crowd in front of Demetrio Antonio's house, because it is near a jeepney stop.

Because I have met with Demetrio several times, he smiled at me and raised his hand.

"Ou!" he cried, when he saw me. His wife was sitting on a round wooden chair. She wore her black one-piece dress. Her grayish hair was bundled at the back of her head as usual.

A wound 20 cm or 25 cm in length runs at the back of his short and stout neck. A Japanese sword did it. His flesh sank inward in line there.

He escaped from Lipa when it became so dangerous there. He tried to go to Bolo Island in Taal Lake where there is no Japanese presence. He ran away to the suburb of Lipa with his wife and two children. But when he came back to his house to take some rice left in it, the Japanese Imperial Army captured him and put him with twenty-six other men who were also captured while they were leaving the town. They were brought to the side of the well and stabbed with bayonets. Then, they were thrown into the well. As he was the last in the line, he was used test a samurai and thrown into the well. The soldiers threw down soil on them. He survived because he managed to breathe.

I wondered how Mr. Antonio could have survived, when I saw the wound inflicted by a samurai on his neck (photo is courtesy of the Forum to Reflect upon the War Victims in the Asia-Pacific Region and Engrave It in Our Minds).

"Even though the Japanese massacred Filipinos, they claim many excuses. While I could survive, those victims must have grudge against the Japanese, because they were innocent," Mr. Antonio said.

His wife then spoke as if she had waited for the end of his narrative: "I cannot understand why they blame the orders. I am so angry that I cannot stay still here. Why are they saying such an excuse even though they killed the people in another country? Where is their feeling of regret?"

Demetrio Antonio, the man stabbed with a
samurai at the back of his neck

"You are an acquaintance of my cousin, Mr. Magaling. Ten members of the Magaling family were killed including the parents and infants. And when the Japanese soldiers learned that my husband was still alive even though he was cut on his neck, they pursued him and tried to kill him. I can never forgive them," she said.

"If the Japanese soldier who cut my neck with a samurai sword comes here to apologize to me, I will welcome him. But . . . "

His wife interrupted him. "I hate him. I don't want to see him," she said.

"You should not be angry anymore," he said as if to reprimand her.

"Why do you say so? Why can you stay quiet, even though you were almost killed?" she said.

They started disputing. He later backed down reluctantly with a smile.

His wife spoke again: "If I see the Japanese soldier appears in front of us, I might collapse in anger. He is responsible for the fact that my husband was almost killed though he was innocent. During that time, I worry for my husband whether he would live or die, because I have children. He could not move his neck at all. I was worried everyday while I was holding my baby in my arms. Do the Japanese understand the anguish of women like me? Though my husband survived, many Filipino men were killed and many women became widows."

"I oppose the visit of my husband to Japan when he was invited there."

He talked on his experience during the war for the audience in Japan, when the members of Forum to Reflect upon the War Victims in the Asia-Pacific Region and Engrave It in Our Minds invited him in the summer of 1998.

"Because someone said the former Japanese soldier would go there to kill him when the soldier will know that he was testifying on his experience in Japan and say that he was cut on his neck," she said.

"But I did believe in it. I would be unfortunate if I would be killed in Japan, even though I had survived the war. I felt at ease when I came back here safely," he said.

"What's your impression of Japan?" I asked.

"The current generation of people there looked so different from those Japanese during the war who were cruel. Those Japanese soldiers haven't died yet; it is strange that they have changed so suddenly. Perhaps the Japanese can change their minds easily. But I cannot easily forget what had happened in the past and I cannot change my mind so easily, either," he said.

They might come back to capture me

I went to Barangay San Carlos by tricycle. Ms. Romana Lajarca was a single lady and sews clothes every day using her sewing machine in her home. But she was out for lunch when I arrived there. She was not in the house of her younger sister, too. I had to wait for her because her sister went out to look for her.

Just before the Japanese Army attacked Barrio San Carlos, men in the village evacuated to safer places, leaving their women and children behind. But those Japanese soldiers attacked the barrio and searched every house. Then they killed the women and children who stayed in the barangay.

Four Japanese soldiers entered her house abruptly and captured two of her elder sisters and her. They brought her sisters to a nearby river. Her younger sister was able to run away, but her elder sisters were killed by being stabbed with bayonets. She was also stabbed deeply and fell on the ground. And she was kicked into the river.

Soon she arrived. Her brown narrow face looks withered and had lost its gloss. I asked her health condition. She said in her low voice, "I have no illness in particular. Perhaps because I cannot live without working with my sewing machine with no rest."

"Do you believe that the Japanese were permitted to kill anybody as long as they were ordered? Did their officer really order them to kill even children and babies? Even though they were ordered, they could not have killed children if they had human heart. But they killed. All the Japanese soldiers are seriously responsible.

"I managed to survive. But one of my younger brothers did not return from that day. Even now we don't know where he was killed.

"I hate the Japanese. But not all Japanese. I am angry and cannot forgive those Japanese who turned the Philippines into a battlefield and did whatever they liked. But I do not feel angry toward younger Japanese. I think all of those Japanese men should go to hell because they acted like devils."

I apologized to her as a Japanese who had also served during the war.

"No, you must not apologize to me because you did not participate in the massacres. Don't worry."

Several middle-aged men were listening to our conversation at the window and the door. And they chatted with each other while they were looking at me. He must have been in the Philippines, though he said he had not been here."

I could not understand what they said. Francisco, my interpreter, heard them and told me about it.

"Do you have any message for those surviving Japanese soldiers?" I asked.

"Do you want me to say any message to those surviving Japanese soldiers . . . ?" she did not finish her sentence.

"You should say what you want to say," one of the women in her house told her.

"I am scared," she said.

"Why are you scared?" I asked.

"The Japanese now are not the same with those Japanese in the past. You should say what you want to say," her younger sister said to encourage her.

"I cannot say. If the former Japanese soldiers read his book, they might come back here to capture me."

"We will help you," the women said unanimously. Laughter was heard somewhere.

But she kept her silence firmly.

God's Teaching: Forgive

When I went to the house of barangay captain in Antipolo to have permission for my research, he said that his daughter-in-law's father was killed by the Japanese in Pamintahan.

I listened to her story. She has vivid eyes, making her look more beautiful.

"I was only two months old in my mother's womb when my father was killed in Pamintahan, I don't know about him at all. Before, I hated and was angry at the Japanese who killed my father. But I have forgiven them. It's only now that I remember my hardships in the past, while I am talking to you. When my father was killed, four of my uncles on my father side were also killed.

After my father's death, my mother went to work as a maid in a big store. She brought me there. I started working, like my mother, in that house at a very young age. I had no time to play and I had no salary. They just gave me meals.

My mother got married again five years after my father had died. I managed to graduate only from elementary school. If my father had not died, perhaps I could have finished high school at least."

Her mother, Mrs. Consolacion Cuenca, lives in a house at some distance from the street. She already has some white hair . . . looked dry. But her white face has a shapely nose, reminding one of her youthful beauty.

"I will never forget the day when my husband was killed. He went out with others to a seminary in Carmel early in the morning. He never came back. Because a survivor told us that everybody had been killed, we ran away with my four-year-old child, though I was pregnant. I thought that even my child would be killed.

"Though I hate the Japanese, I was so scared. I want to take revenge at them, but I had to raise my children. I could do nothing, though I was so angry.

"After my husband was killed, it was very hard for me. I worked as a maid with my daughter. She suffered a lot because she was only a small child.

"I married my cousin five years after my husband was killed. I was still young and had another chance at marriage then."

"I am still angry at the Japanese. My husband would still be alive now if he was not killed. But I am trying to forgive the Japanese little by little, because it is the teaching of God," she said.

"Japanese Imperial Army soldiers tried to kill all the men in Antipolo because they could not distinguish guerrillas from civilians?" I said.

"That's so cruel. I hate the officer who gave that order. It is very selfish," she said.

"Do you have something to say to those surviving Japanese?" I asked.

"They should compensate us for the damage: they've done besides, they killed other people," she said.

"Though you demand compensation from the individual soldiers, you cannot receive anything. You must demand from the Japanese government, because it assumed the supreme responsibility for the war," I said.

She nodded a little and raised her head, "Are you really a Japanese?"

"Yes, I am, but . . . "

"This is the first time for me to meet a Japanese after the Liberation, I feel pain in my heart. I feel like being suffocated," she said.

"Please feel at ease. I have no weapon," I jokingly said to her. She smiled a little."

A Gentle Husband

Mrs. Lolita Alcaraz's house in Barangay Antipolo wasn't easy to locate. I had asked a lot of people before I finally found it near a cemetery.

I talked with Lolita in their small living room. She was short and had a rounded face. Her husband accompanied her as I conducted my interview. He was also short. She married him two years after her first husband was killed in Pamintahan.

"My husband, my father, and two of my brothers were killed in Pamintahan," she began.

"On the 26th, a day before the massacre, a barrio captain told the villagers, 'The Japanese Imperial Army will give us passes. We can freely go anywhere without fear of checkpoints, once we have the passes issued by them.' That's why my husband went to the seminary, the meeting place with other villagers from Anilao and Antipolo, the following morning. But on the 28th, we came to know that all of them were killed. I have been married only for a week. I ran away with the other villagers at once.

"I heard that some of the women went to the camp of the Japanese Army. 'Return our husbands'; they said. But I did not go there; I evacuated to Ibaan [Batangas]. They would have killed me if I complained to them."

Pamintahan, Lipa. The bodies of the husband of Lolita Alicaras, her father, and two of her brothers were thrown in this mountain stream.

"The Japanese soldiers were so cruel. They killed my husband although I had just been married with him. But I don't mean that all of the Japanese soldiers were cruel. The previous soldiers were kind, but those who replaced them were very cruel," her eyes started shining with tears," she said.

"You said that they killed all the men because they could not tell who were guerrillas. It is not the kind of action that human beings can do. We just started living happily because he was a gentle husband," she said while wiping her tears.

"My mother also suffered, because my father and my brothers were killed, although they worked for her. We suddenly became widows," she kept on wiping tears with her fingers and palm while sobbing.

"What do you want to tell those Japanese who took part in the massacre in Pamintahan?" I asked.

"I want to ask them: How do they feel now that they killed so many innocent Filipinos? Are you really sorry?"

"Some of them have regrets. But others don't regret."

"Do they? You mean there are those who do not feel ashamed even though they had killed innocent people?" he said.

I aimed my tape recorder at her husband.

"Though the war happened long ago, God is looking down on us and knows who are guilty," he said.

"Are you still angry at the Japanese?" I asked.

"No, I am not angry at the Japanese anymore," she said in low voice. Her tears had stopped finally.

"My husband, father, and two of my brothers were killed. But I decided to forgive the Japanese because I believe in God,"

"Are you a Catholic?" I asked.

"Yes, I am," her husband nodded simultaneously.

From their window, I saw many children and adult villagers had gathered outside their house. Perhaps they were curious at the Japanese who had suddenly arrived.

"PLEASE DON'T EXPOSE OUR PAST WRONGDOINGS"

The Massacre Batallion

I met with Kinzo Sakagami in a coffee shop in front of the JR railway station located in the center of the prefecture.

"What's your impression of your stay in the Philippines?" I asked.

"I remember the bombing by the U.S. Forces when they attacked us in Lipa Airfield. Some of my comrades were injured in that bombing. I also remember that we starved when we retreated in the mountains," he said.

"Did you participate in the guerrilla subjugation in Lipa?" I asked.

His body stiffened for a moment as if he stopped breathing. "No, I didn't. During the time of the subjugation in Lipa, I was on patrol in Tanauan, because the Americans have already landed. I believe that U.S. Forces were already in Calamba," he said.

"The Japanese Army also conducted guerrilla subjugation in the barrios somewhere in the mountains of Tanauan. Didn't you participate in them?" I asked.

"No, I don't know that at all. But anyway, the guerrillas were our enemies," he said.

"Why did the Filipinos fight against the Japanese Army at the risk of their lives?" I asked.

"We did nothing wrong," he said.

"Food? The Japanese Army must have brought a lot of food from Manchuria when we moved from there."

"How many days did you sustain yourself with it? Did you bring vegetables and meat, too?"

"No, it was not possible, maybe."

"During the end of the war, Japan lost her control of the sea and could not transport food anymore. Because we could not live without supplies, I would have to steal food if I was in Batangas during the war. But if we think of it now, forty-six years after the war, is it reasonable for Filipinos to be hostile to the Japanese Imperial Army?"

"You are right, but . . . "

"Do you think that you did anything wrong to those Filipino war victims?" I asked.

"I feel pity for them," he said.

"Do you feel pity for them. Don't you think that it is necessary to apologize to them?" I asked.

"Yes, I think so. But we cannot go there if the residents in Lipa are still angry at us."

"Have you told your experience in the war to your family?" I asked.

"But the youth are not interested in those experience in the war. But all the member of the veterans group believes that we must not be involved in a war. We included the resolution to act against any war, which is related with Japan, in the oath in our memorial service."

– The memorial service for your comrade is important. But why don't you think on those Filipino victims even though their land was made a battlefield. There are still many victim of war. They are living with scars and wounds inflicted with Japanese sword and bayonet on their bodies. Some of them are only survivors in their families after all of their family members were killed," I said.

"Until now, we just have just thought on ourselves and we have not considered them at all," he said.

"By the way, what is the objective of your veterans' group? Is it for memorial services or just for friendship?" I asked.

"In the beginning, it was mainly for memorial services. Because some dead comrades had not returned to the Yasukuni Shrine yet. And we did not feel like drinking. But as we were getting older, we decided to go sight-seeing together with those comrades gathering from various areas in Japan," he said.

"Why did you change the name of your veterans group to The Corps Veterans Group, even though it was a gathering for the Airfield Battalion? This current name is actually for the corps during their campaign in Manchuria before they were transferred to the Philippines," I said.

"The Airfield Battalion was notorious as a corps responsible for the massacres. This is why our veterans group was founded only recently—six or seven years ago. Many of our comrades were convicted as war criminals," he said.

"Is it possible for you to propose an apology for the war victims in the Philippines to your veterans group?" I asked.

"It will be difficult. Many members believe that our comrades were killed by the guerrillas. They think that there is no need to apologize to the guerrillas since they were attacked by those guerrillas," he said.

"If the Japanese Imperial Army had not invaded the Philippines, there would be no guerrilla activities. At least, is it possible to include the words—"pray for those Filipino and Americans who lost their lives in the battlefields" in your oath use during the memorial service, so that we can avoid a fight with each other anymore," I said.

"I don't know if we can . . . "he spoke evasively.

Beautiful Girls in a Well

The mountains north of Tokyo were light brown in early spring, just before the first leaves of trees come out. The house of Itsuo Kaji was in a quiet residential area in a middle-sized city surrounded by hills.

When I pushed the button of a door bell on the front door, an old man with a bloated face appeared. He was Kaji-san.

"What's your unforgettable experience during the war?" I asked.

"My experience in the Philippines is subjugation. We went to a village, gathered about twenty young and beautiful girls. And we brought them back and locked them up in a house. Though I didn't play with them, the rest of us abused them. Then, our officers changed their mind and decided to reduce the number of the girls. We reduced them to twelve or thirteen girls. It means that we threw seven or eight girls into a well to kill them. Later on, when a newly drafted soldier was guarding them, the remaining girls ran away when he fell asleep.

"In another occasion, we killed four persons, parents and their children, with guns after making them stand in a line. For the charge that they were spies for the U.S. Forces. Because some of them are tall and others short, our bullets hit various places on those in the behind, even though. we aimed at the chest of the man in front.

"When we went to a farmer's house after a subjugation to look for eggs, a child about six years old was lying and groaning. His gut popped out from his belly, but I could do nothing for him. I still remember him vividly," he said.

"Do you remember the time when this subjugation was conducted?" I asked.

"When the war was about to end, because we were near Mt. Malipuyo.

"We conducted a big subjugation in a village at the foot of Mt. Malipuyo at the time. There might be 1,000 residents there. Gonzales, the tiniente del barrio, was ordered by the Japanese Imperial Army to gather the residents in an elementary school. Though I didn't participate, they started killing those residents when it was dark. Everybody, even women and children, were killed, we were ordered to do so," he said.

"Do you sometimes feel you want to apologize to the Filipinos?" I asked.

"Yes, I have. I have a feeling that we committed terrible acts.

"But during the war, the Japanese Imperial Army was cruel not only to the enemy but also to their own soldiers. When we retreat from a cave in Mt. Malipuyo, they left those wounded soldiers behind because they could not walk. It was so cruel."

"Even now I have nightmares on the war. In one such nightmare, I was caught between rocks but an American fighter plane attacked me. I cried and cried, calling for my mother. Then, I woke up," he said.

"Do you remember what happened in the past?" I asked.

"I remember it when I watch the television program on the Gulf War. We were also attacked by the United States like that.

The congressmen are now arguing if Japan will send Self-Defense Force to foreign countries in our Diet. I agree to send troops. Their discussion in the Diet is too slow, they should decide on it faster to send the troop."

"You might think that young people will become victims if Japan participate in a war with neglecting the constitution. But the present war is different from those in the past."

While we chatted on casual matters, I asked his hobby and he said, "I go and bet for boat racing from time to time."

I asked if he could win and he answered with a faint smile on his face.

"No, I cannot. But I go and bet somehow," he said.

Possessed

When I visited the apartment of Shoichi Miyazaki, he allowed me to enter a small room facing south.

"We entered Lipa from Manila. We then guarded the airfield in Lipa. But we had to retreat by the end of March as U.S. Forces are fast approaching. Before we retreated, we bombed all the bridges. Perhaps we destroyed forty or fifty bridges all in all. At midnight before we retreated, we brought oil drums containing gasoline and placed them one can per three houses. And we burned down the town of Lipa, and then retreated to Mt. Malipuyo. It was March 28 when we set fire. When we arrived at Mt. Malipuyo, nobody was there. Those who arrived earlier went back to Lipa, for another attack. The commander of our army corps had ordered them. The commander of our battalion was killed in this attack. It was a foolish order, I think," he said.

He retreated from Mt. Malipuyo on April 29. He told me eagerly the details of the defeat before he arrived at Mt. Banahaw where his troop regrouped. He said that the number of soldiers in that corps had been reduced to one-tenth from 800 soldiers, before they arrived at Mt. Banahaw.

"Our battalion, the 86th Airfield Battalion became famous as a massacre unit, though the subjugation was conducted upon the order by the head of our army corps. Because the order is to kill even women and children, many of solders were charged as war criminals.

131

When I think of it's as if we were possessed by it now, in those days. We did what we can never do in ordinary situation. But we had a little of normal feeling at least. During one of those subjugation, a man approached me with bringing his ID, after he failed to run away. Usually we stabbed those men down without hesitation. But I allowed him go secretly.

Another incident that I cannot forget is the one in the village on the foot of Mt. Malipuyo. The captain of other troop called me and ordered to blast an hall in an elementary school by placing bomb on the corner of the building, when they would gather the resident in that building. I claimed that it was impossible to kill all of the residents in such away. But the captain ordered to me to blast. Then, my direct senior officer came back, and the plan was cancelled. The residents were brought to a mountain stream and killed with bayonets there."

"When I think on 'guerrilla subjugation' now, it seems cruel. But the Japanese were also suffered a certain degree of damage. When we placed a sentry, he disappeared before we could notice. And a doctor in the town of Malvar offered a car made by Packard to the Japanese Imperial Army. But actually he was a principal member of the guerrilla. We could not be off our guard any time."

"You may want to ask me why we killed old men, children, and even babies. But we had no room to think on it. The orders had to be followed absolutely in the army. One cannot understand it, unless he has fought in the battlefield. The hearts of the soldiers were like devils. I think the residents suffered a lot. We were almost crazy there. We did whatever we were ordered to do, even though it went beyond our imagination in the ordinary situation.

They threw down the bodies of those killed in Solok in the forest of Quemuros in this river.

"Then, while I was thinking I might die anytime, I also thought that I would never die. But because I wanted to wear clean underwear when I die, I changed my underwear everyday I had a lot of underwear made of silk cloth for parachute.

"This is just my personal opinion. Most of those who committed wrongdoings. For example, raping were killed in the war."

He sent me a New Year greeting card with this message:

> *As I told you last year, I cannot forget the incidents that happened around Lipa even now. Some of my comrades are still scared of being charged as war criminals. Please do not expose our past wrongdoings carelessly.*

We Did Commit Something Slightly Wrong

I found Harukichi Mukoyama's house. It was a fifteen – minute walk from the train station. Though it was a simple duplex along a narrow alley, its columns and window frames are well-polished.

I listened to the remembrance of Mukoyama-san's story at the entrance of his house. He was a short, old man; his hair is already white.

"I do not remember what happened in this period clearly. It's the truth. Maybe I lost my memory because of the heat of the southern country. Also, I got sick of dysentery and had to lie in a cave, too." he said.

"What about your experience in guerrilla subjugation?" I asked.

"We gathered military currency by attacking a village and searching the houses in it. We were not paid our salaries at all; we could not buy anything. We also collected valuable things: watches, rings, and others. When we attacked another village, one of the airplanes of the U.S. Forces found us. They bombed us. It was a terrible experience for me."

"Do you ask me the reason why we subjugated the Filipino resident? It was because we were ordered to kill even children if they were above ten years old. The reason was that they might inform the activities of the Japanese Imperial Army to the U.S. Forces.

But it was difficult to kill people even though they did not fight against us. When we were not involved in any battle and we didn't experience that we were really in a war, the military police sent seven guerrilla suspects to us, so that we would execute them. Our officer told us, 'Because you have no experience in killing any man, we will conduct the exercise of killing so that you could become courageous.' Somebody had already dug up holes in a coconut farm, and the men stood beside the halls with their eyes covered with clothes. We fixed our bayonets on our rifles and stabbed them. But my bayonet penetrated into the body only 3 cm deep. Because I was so confused and my elbow was not correctly positioned on my body, I could not press the bayonet strongly to the body. I was so frustrated. The soldiers were standing in three lines and they stabbed and killed the suspects in turn. We threw them into the hole. But I did not remember if we covered the bodies with soil.

While we were in fierce battle, we might kill the enemies because we were so agitated. But when we were in normal situation, it was very difficult to kill."

"Do you ask me if I did something wrong to Filipinos?" I asked.

"No, I don't think so at all. I did nothing wrong to them.

I was just recruited with a simple letter from the army. And I did nothing wrong. Those low-ranked soldiers like me were just ordered by the superior officers at their will," he said.

"Do you ask me again if I really committed nothing wrong?" I asked.

"What do you mean? You may ask me in that way because I belonged to the guard unit. Of course, we did commit something wrong a little. But it was war. Our enemy was similarly cruel to us," he said.

Proud Still

Though I visited him the previous day, he was not around today. Then, I called him up for an appointment and visited his house again. His name was Chikara Okawa. He was a college student during the war, but he joined the army without asking the postponement of service.

"I was shot on my left leg by the machine gun of an American fighter plane in Lipa. When my leg was recovering somewhat, the bell of the wired telephone rang in the headquarters of our corps while I was there. When I hang off the phone, the person on the other side of the line shouted to me."

"Is the commander of your battalion there? I need to talk to him," he said.

"May I know who's on the line?" I asked.

"This is the adviser for the corps. Hurry up," he said.

He shouted to me again. He was already behaving crazy. His order was to attack back to Lipa from where we had just retreated after burning it down. The order was very absurd because the tanks of the U.S. Army were fast approaching toward us.

As I was wounded on my leg, I went there on the back of a donkey. Though the commander of our battalion said to me, "You should go back", I couldn't. When we came to a mountain stream, I fell off from the back of the donkey. The commander told me, "I brought an important document with me. You should bring it back to the cave." He saved me from this rushing."

"I have good memories of Filipinos, too. The family of a dentist invited me to their house in Lipa. I could spend a good evening with them. I sung songs to the accompaniment of piano there. One day, the brother-in-law of that dentist was arrested by the military police in Lipa for the suspicion of guerrilla activity. I happened to meet with his nephew on a road, and they asked to me to save him. Though I was not an officer, I went to military police to save his life. But he was executed. When I met with that child, he said directly to me, "You are a powerless person". I was shocked too much.

When I was confined as a prisoner of war, we were summoned for verification using witnesses. I noticed the dentist and his wife were passing with looking at my face. I believed firmly that I would be condemned as a war criminal. But contrary to my fear, the officer of the U.S. Forces summoned me and said, 'Your charge as a war criminal was cleared. You must prepare for your return to Japan immediately.' I was very glad. The dentist and his wife remembered my face and they must testify my innocence.

I just remember that an old farmer came to our headquarters and claimed something. When we asked him about his complain with the help of an interpreter because we could not understand his Tagalog, he said some soldiers killed his carabao and ate it. When I went to the site, it smelled good. Because those soldiers did not belong to our unit and we were not military police, we could not punish them. We gave him a big box of cigarettes as compensation.

After that incident, the military police gave strict orders not to plunder from the residents. But because food was not supplied, we could not live if we'll follow the order. The plundering of food was a necessary evil for us," he said.

"Do you wish to apologize to the war victims in the Philippines?" I asked.

"Yes, I have, because we killed even noncombatants, women and children. But I think that the compensation was already paid by the Japanese government," he said.

"Do you say that it was only compensation between governments and even 1 peso was not paid to the victims. But perhaps those victims will not forgive us even though we apologized to them seriously as long as the Japanese government does not work for it. So, we just have to keep away from this issue. Although I did not commit anything, I do not feel like going to Lipa."

"Do you ever attend a veterans meeting?" I asked.

No, I do not want to attend, though I gave donation at least. I could not agree with them. When I attended the gathering once, one of them proudly said that he had slashed how many residents in some village. When I said in a loud voice 'It is imprudent to say such an evil conduct,' the atmosphere was spoiled. I will never attend it anymore.

"Who was responsible for that war? Some claim Hideki Tojo was responsible. But if he had not escalated the war, the common people would have become angry and rioted. I think those individual citizens in Japan were also responsible for the war. And it is not necessarily correct to say that the Emperor was not responsible for it.

I Deserved to be Killed

I met with Tadayoshi Kawabe in a room of a building in a big city in Kansai (western Japan). He answered my questions while he had to reply to some occasional phone calls.

"I was a driver for the commander of our corps, I stayed in the vicinity of the dugout used as our headquarter. A tank of U.S. Force stopped in the front of our dugout with loud noise and it opened a flame-thrower toward it. I saw the blaze blew out from the entrance in the opposite direction. It had a tremendous firepower."

"And I can never forget the time when I was wounded on my arm. Because we had to stay in shallow dugouts, we had to vent our bodies deeply to avoid danger. In noontime, U.S. Forces started massive attack. My rifle was broken into two while I placed it vertically. I noticed that I had been thrown away with two or three soldiers when I regained my consciousness. My left arm was terribly wounded with fragment of a cannonball.

When I was confined as a prisoner of war, I was bemauled by a woman officer of U.S. Force. While we were working to cut grass, the woman officer came to me and threw a cigarette with lipstick mark beside of me intentionally. I stepped on it to crash. She got angry while pointed at me. She might think that I ruined her present. I was brought to the camp office and punished. I had to endure for three days only drinking water. It was terribly hard for me because it was too hot."

"Did you take part in some guerrilla subjugation?" I asked.

"Yes, I have some experience. I stabbed the back of a resident with a bayonet and threw him down into a well. We also attacked a village, caught old men, women and children, and confined them in a few houses. Then we set fire on the houses to burn them to death.

One day, we set fire on a house with raised floor. But a hand stuck out from the house to put the fire off. There was a woman holding a child in that house. I said to her to come out, but she could not understand what I was saying. When I set fire on the house, she put it off again. And then she sneaked down under some table or something. She should better come out, but she didn't come out, perhaps because she was afraid of the Japanese. When the fire spread to her hair from her body, she was burnt to death.

Maybe because I killed the civilian Filipinos during the subjugation, I still have nightmares. After I had talked on my experience like this, I ran and ran from the enemy in my nightmare. Then I will wake up with suffering. Then I think, 'I am lucky, it was only a nightmare.'"

"Many of your comrades keep what you did in the Philippines a secret?"

"It is not a right attitude. When I am wearing a short-sleeved shirt, I show my wound on my arm to Filipinos and say nonchalantly, 'This wound was inflicted in the battlefield in the Philippines.' Filipinos were astonished a moment, but they just react to it by saying 'You have such an experience,' and do not take your revenge on me. If they do revenge me, they have a right to do so. It is because the Japanese Army did more than that in the Philippines. We did whatever you might imagine. Theft, arson, torture, and murder. We did everything we might be charged with in Japan. But we returned alive without getting killed. And I have lived more than forty years now. I will not complain if I am killed now. Because we killed them, they have a right to kill us. It is a matter of course. But Filipinos do not kill us. They forgive me by saying 'It happened during the war.' I deserve it.

But my former comrades try to hide what we did in the past. They are cowards. I believe we must reveal what we had done in the past. We must not repeat such a tragedy.

By the way, those young Japanese in the Philippines seem to engage in wrongdoings. They deceive and sell women and threaten them like the Yakuza. If they behave so, Filipinos would think the Japanese are bad people even today, same as their soldiers were during the war. I hope those Japanese would be careful about their behavior."

"Do you want to know what's my impression of the war, when I look back at the past? We did stupid things. We only followed whatever our senior officers ordered us.

It's good Japan was defeated. Had she won, the Japanese people would be heavily taxed to maintain her bases abroad. People in the occupied countries would not be silent. Japan would have to maintain an army in those countries. It would have been costly. And people in Korea and Taiwan would have continued to suffer."

"Yes, I talk on my cruel experience during the war in the Philippines to my family. I tell them whatever I experienced including the massacres. I tell them, 'My hands are stained with the blood of Filipinos.' I also revealed my experience when I threw down the residents into a well, I threw a grenade down into it because one of the victims shouted, 'Bakayaro!' (Damn you!) at me."

Are you afraid that my children might think I was cruel and hate me if I tell them? No, they won't. My daughter understands in her own way that war is cruel. This is the reality. If I do not tell them the truth, they will not understand war's vicious aspects. We must tell them the truth so that we heed not fight a war anymore.

JAPANESE CLAIM SELFISH REASONING

One out of Fourteen Sisters

I got off a jeepney in front of the house of Juan Guzman in barrio Lumban.

"When the massacre began on March 4, there was no Makapili living in this barrio. Those Makapili came from a faraway town. Because they informed the Japanese Army that the residents in Lumban and Solok had relations with guerrillas, the massacre was started. This is what I think.

Anyway, even though the Japanese tried to kill all the residents, do they still claim we were guerrilla suspects even now? Filipinos would never accept such reasoning. It is because my parents, my elder brother, my elder sister and her husband, and their children and my younger sisters were killed in the massacre. We lost nine persons all in all. The residents were completely innocent. My elder brother was still single then.

My elder sister, her husband and their small children were brought to the forest in Quemuros. Because they were at the back among those who were brought there, they ran away desperately while holding their daughters in their arms, when they noticed Japanese soldiers began surrounding them armed with rifles with attached bayonet. Luckily they survived."

"I cannot understand why it was impossible for the Japanese soldiers to ask to their superiors officer back, 'Why was it necessary to kill even women and children?' Even though they claim that they must obey absolutely the orders issued by their senior officers. It is impossible for the Filipino victims to understand the strict conditions within the Japanese Imperial Army.

Only less than one hundred people could survive among one thousand seven hundred residents in barrio Lumban. It was the biggest massacre among the barrios in Lipa."

"Is it true that some of those remaining Japanese soldiers who were stationed in Lipa want to apologize to us? . . . I am willing to accept their apology. My wife will accept it, too."

He glanced at his plump wife who brought cups of coffee.

His wife had fourteen sisters. But thirteen among them between three to sixteen years old, were all killed.

"But I can only accept the apology from those who want to some apologize voluntarily, because they know that they committed some wrongdoing. Maybe there are those who don't know it."

"Please tell those surviving Japanese soldiers. Tell them that they should not be afraid of us. Please visit our barangay to apologize from your heart. If possible, please help us in the development of our barangay as a form of their apology. The Japanese government claims they paid compensation to the Philippine government, but even one peso was not paid to those war victims."

Seven Comfort Women

It was the first time for me to meet with Mr. Antonio Birgonio. He had a handsome face with good-shaped nose and wore a white and navy blue stripe T-shirt.

On March 4, 1945 when the people in Lumban were gathered in an elementary school in Solok and massacred in the forest of Quemuros, he was brought to a mountain from the schoolyard to be used in forced labor.

"I was just fourteen years old, but I was forced to work for the Japanese Imperial Army together with about seventy men. My first duty was to bring rice bags from Solok to a tunnel used by the Japanese Imperial

Army. When the work was done and I was going to go home, I was forced to dig a tunnel for their bastion. It was very hard.

The hardship during that period was that I was not paid. Moreover I have nothing to eat. The Japanese soldiers cooked rice but they just gave us potatoes only, even though they were not working. Though we were hungry, we were forced to bring the box of ammunitions up the mountain. Though I thought several times that I must run away, I could not make up my mind because we were threatened. They said "We will consider you as guerrillas if you run away, and will cut you down on the spot. I could not made up my mind because I was just fourteen years old then. I was forced to work for one month with no payment.

Many were killed after the work was done, but we survived by running away. When U.S. Forces made an air raid, I ran away with seven other friends, because the Japanese soldiers hurriedly hid. I was lucky."

"When the people had been gathered in the elementary school to be killed in Quemuros, young beautiful women were selected and brought to the mountain with us.

"I saw them from time to time while I was in the mountain. When I asked them, "What are you doing", they put their finger on the lips and answered with their eyes that they could not answer anything. The Japanese soldiers were watching them at a short distance. Seven women were forced to work as comfort women from this town, Lumban. I cannot reveal their names, though

I know them. There were more than twenty comfort women there all in all."

"Among our family, my grandparents, uncle and aunt were killed. I wanted to take revenge against the Japanese then. I refrained from it because I was young. But I would have been a guerrilla if I had been about twenty years old."

"Is it true that some of those Japanese soldiers are still alive? he asked.

The Japanese made terrible mistakes. They even killed those innocent children. What do they think of it now? I want to know what they really think."

The Cry at the Atomic Bomb Park

You will enter Barangay Solok when you cross over a mountain stream flowing from Mt. Malarayat. The forest of Quemuros, where the Japanese Army massacred the residents, is located in the outskirts of this barangay. There is another massacre site in Bulihan three kilometers downstream from it. (This place was also called as Ke Impyerno in Tagalog language, meaning "hell".) This place was used as evacuation site during the war. But they say that it has become a wilderness again and there is no road going there.

I have met Marcelino Magaling many times. He became an orphan when he was only seven years old and evacuated to Bulihan. The Japanese massacred the residents ten members of his family, including his parents, brothers and sisters, were killed there. He was also stabbed on his chest with a bayonet and the wounds pierced through his body from the back to the chest, but U.S. Forces brought him to the Philippine General Hospital in Manila. After six months of hospitalization, he regained his health.

"Many people including our family evacuated to Bulihan to avoid calamities in the war. The Makapili reported to the Japanese Imperial Army that they were guerrillas. Makapili wanted to have better life by selling fellow Filipinos.

The Japanese Imperial Army was barbarous. I am sure that they tried to kill everybody by blindly believing what Makapili claimed, because they were insane while they were fighting a losing battle. Many of those victims could never accept the excuse of the Japanese.

Those Japanese soldiers who stabbed us with bayonets say they had to obey the orders and the orders by senior officers were absolute for them and so they were not responsible. But was it really true? They exercised Judo on me while I was crying for fear. They threw me down to the ground. They tried to kill me by stabbing me with a bayonet four times. I was only seven years old. Was it really conducted by an order? . . . Wasn't there any will of the soldier that tried to kill a child? . . . The youngest among my brothers was only two years old when he was killed. Did they stab him with a bayonet by saying to themselves that it was what they were ordered to do and they must obey it?

When I was invited to Japan, I met a former Japanese soldier who had taken part in the massacre in Pamintahan in Lipa. He said he could not have disobeyed the order by his senior. But even though they were ordered, those soldiers were still responsible as long as they killed our countrymen with bayonets directly by themselves. Of course, the commander had the biggest responsibility because he issued the order. But I doubt whether the Japanese senior officer really ordered to kill even babies."

He visited Japan in the summer of 1989 on the invitation of the Forum to Reflect upon the War Victims in the Asia-Pacific Region and Engrave It in Our Minds to talk about his experience during the war in several places in Japan.

"I will accept from my heart those Japanese who want to apologize. It is peaceful time now and I am Christian. And also because I am working for a church in our area.

Both Japanese and we Filipinos are human beings. Before I went to Japan, I only thought about Japanese negatively, because I had a hard experience. So it was a kind of adventure for me to go to Japan. But in the same time I have an expectation for Japan. When we arrived at Osaka Airport, you and many other people welcomed us. I was very glad. I thought the Japanese are better than I had thought.

It may be different now, but during the time of war Japanese believed that it was a matter of course that they acted loyal to the senior officers who represented. The Emperor and the national flag. So, when they were ordered, they tried to kill all Filipinos. They killed almost all the residents of Barangay Lumban. It was a terrible insanity.

When I went to Hiroshima with other participants and read a poem titled 'Bring back my father, bring back my mother' at the Atomic Bomb Park (Peace Memorial Park), I cried when I remember my parents, sisters, and brothers who were killed.

But I also realized Japanese also suffered from the atomic bombs like us. Anyway, I hope there will be no more war."

Japan Should Pay

Mrs. Apolonia Navarro is already old and her spine is bent. She was stroking the head of a gray dog with her shoulders stooped. Her blind husband was not there. She remarried after her husband was killed.

"When I regained my consciousness, my children were already brought away. They were ten and six years old then. The Japanese army killed and threw them away somewhere. I was wounded on seven places on my body. One of them penetrated my chest but I could survive. Fortunately because I was not stabbed on my belly, my daughter was not killed while I was pregnant with her.

She is my daughter who was in my womb at the time of war.

She introduced a middle-aged woman standing beside a wooden chair. She had not lived with her two years ago. When I first visited her. When did she come back to her?

"After I lost my husband, I lived like a beggar. I had a baby, but I could not work because I was wounded terribly. I even begged in the town of Lipa.

It was not only me who was forced to live miserable life because of the war. Many men were killed in Lipa and its surroundings. Many women became widows and many children lost their fathers. But do you say that the Japanese do not apologize and claim they tried to kill everybody because they could not distinguish who was a guerrilla? Aren't they ashamed as human beings?

"I want to ask those surviving Japanese soldiers. My life has been miserable ever since Japanese conducted the massacre. I became weak and my daughter supports me now. If it's possible, I hope that the Japanese soldiers pay me some compensation. I will be glad if they can do so."

"I want to ask, too."

"I want them to help my mother," her daughter said.

Her daughter continued: "We came back from Mariveles in Bataan to help my mother and father-in-law. My husband is working as a temporary worker to harvest coconuts. His wage is only sixty pesos a day. We don't have our own land or rented farmland. We have to support my children and parents with this daily wage."

"We only have money when he has work to do. And work is not available everyday."

151

Mr. Magaling who guided me to her house explained. Sixty pesos is only two-thirds of the minimum daily wage defined by the government for agricultural workers.

"Please tell them to compensate us," Mrs. Navarro said again with her teary eyes.

"But the issue of compensation will not be solved by individuals unless you demand the government of Japan which must assume all of the responsibility for the war. It will not be solved, even though you demand it to those individual former soldiers," I said.

By saying this to her, I thought, again that this problem could not be solved unless Filipinos start the movement to demand the compensation to the government of Japan.

The Japanese Imperial Army and the U.S. Forces

When I went to Barangay San Antonio Mt. Malarayat was just in front of me. The Japanese Imperial Army had once entrenched itself on that mountain.

I went to Ms. Aleria Pastormayor house, guided by a former barangay captain. As I walked on a coconut farm road I saw the mountains on the right. Her small house is on the left.

When we reached her house, she came out wearing eyeglasses and a check-printed dress. It was the same dress she wore two years ago when I took her picture. She has a shawl on her shoulders, perhaps because she felt somewhat cold. When I compared her face with her image in that picture, I noticed she had lost a lot of vitality.

"Are you still angry at those Japanese who killed your husband?" I asked him.

"Yes of course, I am still angry at them," she said.

"The Japanese soldiers claim they need not apologize to the Filipino war victims because it was war; they will be killed if don't they kill the enemy," I said.

"I beg to disagree. Maybe applies to soldiers, but my husband was just an ordinary civilian. In my opinion, all those Japanese who invaded the Philippines committed crimes. So, it is but natural that they should apologize to the war victims. What they did was almost the same as entering other people's houses depriving them of food without asking permission. Filipinos experienced great difficulties during those times," she said.

"The Japanese soldiers believe that even women and children supported the guerrillas?" I said.

"It was wrong to believe so. Though I supported the guerrillas in my heart, I could do nothing because I have a baby and she was only three months old," she said.

"What's the difference between the Japanese Imperial Army and the U.S. Forces?" I asked.

"The Japanese Imperial Army were so cruel, but the U.S. Forces helped us. When this area was about to become a battlefield between the U.S. Forces and the Japanese Imperial Army, Americans helped us to evacuate. We moved to Ibaan for our safety. In comparison, the Japanese Imperial Army suddenly attacked our barrio and massacred our fellow residents. That is the big difference," she said.

"What do you want to tell those Japanese soldiers?" I asked.

"I am eager to ask those Japanese soldiers, for my peace of mind, why did they kill my husband? I want an answer," she said.

A dry wind was blowing through the coconut trees in the farm.

I visited Eugene Las in his house. He was orphaned by the war because the Japanese Imperial Army killed all members of his family. I found that he had moved from his former house on the left side of the road to that on the right side. He said that he had exchanged his house with that of his cousin.

"I have an unforgettable experience with the Japanese soldiers. It happened the day after they massacred my parents. I went down to the mountain stream where they were thrown. I looked for their remains there. When I was searching for them,—I wanted to see them even though I was only nine years old then—the Japanese soldiers shot me. I ran away as fast as I could. I felt fierce anger against those Japanese who did not care about the feeling of a child who had just lost his parents.

"After my parents were killed, I evacuated with my neighbors. I ran away desperately when someone cried out, 'the Japanese are coming!' I ran and ran because I was so scared. I didn't notice I had already reached Tagaytay. I survived on the generosity of neighbors. But I was so hungry since I only ate once a day.

"After Liberation, I worked as a stay-in houseboy in other people's houses. When I quit from elementary school I was in Grade Two. It is absurd to claim that they killed even women and children because they collaborated with guerrillas. I want to ask the Japanese soldiers if they saw the residents with guns. Without even examining who was a guerrilla, they killed the residents. And yet they still claim that the residents were guerrillas. What harm did the women and children in this barangay do to them? Even though they were not attacked here, they killed may people here. Only crazy people can claim they could not tell whether or not the residents were guerrillas so they tried to kill everybody. I don't know who gave such an order but if they are humane, they would never issue such an order. They would not kill babies, even when they were ordered."

"Do you have any message for those Japanese soldiers who were stationed in Lipa, Batangas during the war," I asked.

"Of course, I have. Even now when I recall the massacre, I still tremble. I hope that those Japanese will not forget that they made me an orphan. That I

155

always think it would have been better if they had not killed my parents."

We then talked about lighter subjects. He lost the paddy field he's tilling two years ago when his landlord sold the land, of which his field was a part. He is now working as a day laborer. He is paid seventy pesos a day. He also said he will earn thirty pesos for every 1,000 coconut that he had peeled.

The Heart of Juan Casanova

When I visited Juan Casanova in his house, he was engaged in a game of jueteng. I saw about ten people in the house. It was my first time to meet him.

"I was twelve at the time. We evacuated to Bulihan. I was with my parents in a small hut. We want to be as far as possible from the effects of the war. But the Japanese soldiers attacked us there. My parents, a younger sister, and three younger brothers were all massacred. Only I survived. When I saw the Japanese soldiers are coming, I ran away with my relatives in desperation. I ran with them to Barrio Dagatan and stayed there for a month until the American arrived.

That night, I learned that my family were all killed. I cried. My parents, my sister and my three brothers all dead! A survivor recalled to me what he saw: the Japanese soldiers caught my family, tied their hands on their backs, and herded them in a place in Bulihan. They emplaced a machine gun so that they could shoot them at will if they attempted to escape. They then brought the villagers, ten persons at a time, to the back of a mountain stream, stabbed them with bayonets and threw them in the river. About three hundred residents died this way.

Now an orphan, I wanted to take revenge against the Japanese soldiers. But I could not do anything because I was so scared. I just hid so that they could not find me.

After Liberation, my uncle took me under his wings. I wasn't able go back to school because school was so far. Instead, I raised pigs, ducks and horses. That's why I can not read and write. But I can write my name. At least I can count money because it is necessary to live. If my parents had not been killed, I could have gone to school."

"Are you still angry at the Japanese? . . . In the beginning I was angry. But later on I decided to forgive them because it happened during the war. So, I do not have any bad feelings to you, either.

"Can you forgive them from the bottom of your heart?" I asked.

"Of course I can, because it is the teaching of God, he said. "

"Do you want to know my message to those Japanese who were stationed in Lipa? They killed all of my family though we lived peacefully. But I have already forgiven them despite the incident. Please tell that to them," he said.

When I was about to leave, he offered lunch. I declined his offer and waited for a jeepney to come.

Before I returned to Manila, I paid a visited to a subcontractor of a Japanese motor company, which has started operating in the suburbs of Lipa. The factory imports electrical parts of cars from Japan and assemble them here and exports them back to Japan. They built the factory here because of cheap labor.

The Japanese president said proudly, "I abide by the minimum wage law. I am a VIP in this town." But his company will more out once the labor cost rises.

CHAPTER 4

TAAL, BAUAN

L ake Taal is located in the north of Batangas City and the small volcanic island in this lake was the safe evacuation place for Filipinos. They say that Filipinos brought all boat on the lake shore to the island so that Japanese soldiers could not come to the islands.

In Taal area, a the southern and eastern sections of this Lake Taal, the Japanese army conducted "guerrilla subjugation" from February 16 to 18, 1945. The Japanese soldiers attacked several barrios, and killed men, women and children indiscriminately and set fire on houses.

And in Bauan, the village next to Batangas City, the Japanese army gathered all the residents in a Catholic church in February 28, 1945. Then they moved women and children to an elementary school but brought male residents to the mansion of wealthy Bautista family, which the Japanese army had been requisitioned and used. According to the testimonies by Filipino in "Records of War Crimes by Japanese Army", 348 residents were confined in the house and blasted with bombs set on the ceiling of the house. When the survivors tried to run away, the Japanese soldiers were surrounding the house and killed them with bayonet and gun.

And the Japanese Imperial Army set fire on houses. They had burned down almost all areas in the town.

This "guerrilla subjugation" was conducted by units belonging mainly to the Battalion of the Infantry

Regiment which was stationed in Cuenca, Batangas at the time. This "Bauan Subjugation" is not recorded in *War History Library,* Vol. 60, *Army Operation "Shun" (2), Decisive in Luzon* nor in *War History of the Infantry Battalion of X Regiment in the Philippines.* But 2nd Lt. Saburo Matsuno listed the names of the units, involved in this "guerrilla subjugation", clearly in the record of the court proceeding against him ("Record of War Crimes by the Japanese Army"). He was executed by firing squad for the responsibility for both of the subjugation.

THEY STARTED IT

Might is Right

I got off the empty train station which stands alone in the wind-swept paddy fields.

Tsutomu Suzuki, a former low-ranking officer, lives near the railway station.

"Though they say the Japanese Army did wrongdoing in the Philippines, it was the guerrillas who started the war. When we were attacked, we couldn't remain passive." He started talking with his narrow brown face stiffened somewhat.

"Perhaps they were angry because the Japanese Imperial Army commandeered food stock or for other reasons. They attacked the small group of Japanese Imperial Army everywhere. Whenever we found dead bodies of our comrades, we interrogated Filipinos to find out who killed them. But they kept silent to our questions and pretended to know nothing. So we decided to kill them because they started this battle.

But actually we did not treat them so cruelly. Because soldiers were proud on how many they cut down in the battlefield, it was exaggerated as if the Japanese Army killed hundreds of enemies. It was a mere exaggeration.

I doubt if the Lipa incident did really happen. It is because we stayed in the house of the town mayor of Lipa for seventeen days to gather the remains of the abandoned comrades. The mayor didn't say anything about the massacre even though he said he had been a former guerrilla leader."

– Filipinos do not say anything impolite to those visitors who came a long way.

"Well, but he didn't even show a sign of it."

"My experience in 'guerrilla subjugation'? I never participated in the subjugation. I was assigned at the regimental headquarters at that time."

"The regimental headquarters were changed into the corps headquarters during that time. And it ordered 'guerrilla subjugation'. It was on January 25, 1945. Of course, you should know it because you are an officer, shouldn't you?"

"No, I don't know about the details."

It is said that Shimbu Corps expelled the residents from the expected battlefield when the 14th Area Army issued the war directive to it: "Make the battlefield uninhabitable". But X Corps tried to subjugate the residents in the expected battlefield when it governed both Laguna and Batangas provinces.

– Why did the X Corps commander try to make the area uninhabitable?

"I don't know. The low-ranked officers like me would never know it."

"You said it was an exaggeration that the existence of mass slaughter in the Philippines. But the corps headquarters ordered the "guerrilla subjugation" while you were a member of it. And they even pressured those units when the units were hesitant. As a result, even the innocent residents were killed.

"I have heard such rumors. But we don't know if it is true."

"You belonged to the X Battalion of the X Infantry Regiment and this battalion conducted the subjugation in Taal and Bauan.

He said nothing.

"By the way, Suzuki. You quoted a proverb 'Might is right' in a magazine for veterans gathering. And you wrote that Japanese were severely criticized by Filipinos because Japan had lost the war, didn't you?

"What I wanted to say was the war tribunal was a sham and even the innocent officers were executed because they are accuse to have committed some crimes through they did not commit any crimes. Such absurdity happened because we had lost the war. If we had won the war..."

"Do you mean to say the resident massacred by the Japanese Army in Calamba, San Pablo, Lipa, and Bauan this incident would have been forgotten, if Japan had won the war?

"I have a complain against those political parties and people who always criticize the bad aspects of the Japanese army, even though they did not sacrifice their lives. This is I have seen thinking since the end of the war. I am angry to those self-righteous people who claim they have been right while they didn't but never have courage to shed their own sweat, tear and lives.

If millions had protested against the war, the Japanese government would not have gone into war. If so, our comrades would not have been killed. But they claim whatever they want to tell after the war. I hate those people.

I do not want any war in the future, but we cannot say there will be no more war. I believe it is necessary for millions of people to stop war in general war."

He said as if he want to express his complaints he had kept in his daily life.

My Fallen Comrades

Though Taiji Yamada was not at home, a middle-aged woman in his neighborhood said he would be back by noon as he went out to his field, when I asked her. As she noticed that I was wondering how I would spent half an hour by that time, she said to me to enter her living room and have a tea. I waited for Yamada-san while chatting with her and eating peas and corns offered by her.

"Do you ask me if I have an experience in 'guerrilla subjugation'? Yes, I have. We went out from Cuenca and subjugated in Taal. Some of my comrades who once served in the Kantogun, an army unit stationed in China, they conducted the subjugation.

Please don't ask me about the details of the subjugation. I might be bashed if I tell you the truth. The surviving members of our unit still annoyed the subjugation they have committed. So some of them do not go to the Philippines for war memorial services by themselves but instead send their sons. They feel guilty and regret. And they have a remorse, which they could not reveal to anyone else. Even we gather for veterans meeting, nobody wants to talk about it. Although some of them start talking about it after a drink . . . ."

"A war makes men abnormal. It changes us to do anything cruel, which cannot be done in a normal situation. What we did there was completely the act of bullying the weak."

"Do you ask me the reason why we killed even women and children . . .? I clearly remember we were

166

ordered to 'kill all Filipinos including women and children' before subjugation in Taal. But when I asked about this order to the officer, who gave us the order, he denied it and said, 'No, I didn't'. It is strange that the officer who gave the order do not remember it while the soldiers clearly remember it."

"And recently I think something is wrong. I hear sometimes the complaints claiming that the war tribunals in the Philippines were completely biased. They use Bai incident as an example in which an innocent soldier was found guilty and executed. It may be true for the case of Chukichi Itoh in the Bai incident, but it is also a fact that we conducted 'guerrilla subjugation' in Bai and killed many Filipinos there. I think it is wrong to claim only the trials were completely wrong while neglecting the existence of subjugation.

And there is one more thing to say. Some say the dead soldiers could not rest in peace because Japan lost the war. But I doubt if they could rest in peace if Japan had won the war. I believe Japan was transformed from militarism to the current society because many of our comrades died in the battlefield."

"Yes, as you have said, we also sacrificed the people of the other countries. We killed Asian people including many Filipinos. Then a new era has arrived."

Later on, I met with Yamada-san again in a small town where he lived. He started talking on his experience on subjugation without hesitation.

"When we were in Cuenca in the foot of Mt. Macorodo, I joined in 'Taal subjugation.' When we entered the village, there were no resident left there as they had already fled away. We burned the houses one by one. We searched for the residents and we found that they hid in a deep valley. They even brought horses there. Before we could capture the residents, the horses ran wild. And while we were taming the horses, the residents ran away. Because they could not go so far away, we looked for them and found them in a bush. We pulled them out and made them stand in line. There were twenty people including men, women and children. We aimed our machine gun at them hidden in the grass, I can never forget a mother falling down holding her baby in her arm.

I remember we covered their bodies with grass after we killed them."

He looked relieved after talking his story and said, "I feel relived as I talked the secret that have kept in my heart for a long time. It is the first time for me to tell it to other people."

How can they go for memorial services while forgetting the past?

After I asked directions to a real estate broker near a bus stop, I could easily find the house of Toyonosuke Yamaoka. He came out to the entrance in a short-sleeved shirt even though it was already early winter. Perhaps his room was warm enough because it was on the seventh floor in a high-rise apartment with plenty of sunshine pouring in.

"Because I was born and grew up in Tokyo, they found me as useful in our unit. I worked as assistant for a personnel administration officer even though I was a fresh recruit. I was not required to join in hard exercises.

After I was dispatched to the Philippines, I also worked for the unit headquarters. So, I need not go and join them in the subjugation activity.

Do you want to know of my unforgettable experience during the war? It is maybe that I was almost get killed. It was when I was staying near Mt. Macolodo. On day we were surrounded by American Forces. The platoon leader left me alone. I fell off into a mountain stream and consciousness in that incident. I remember that night dew was dropped on my face and the moon was shining bright when I gained consciousness. I rejoined of my platoon some two or three days later.

The Japanese Imperial Army were cruel to Filipinos, but it was also cruel to its own soldiers. It executed one of three soldiers they were sent out to subjugation but lost their way. After their mission he was charged of desertion even when the war had already ended."

"Do you ask me for my opinion on the Filipino guerrillas during that time? All of the residents were guerrillas, weren't they? Though I had no chance to have a relation with the local residents, I noticed they were snooping at us secretly. Maybe it goes without saying they looked at us that way because their land was made into a battlefield and their food was stolen. And once they were suspected a guerrillas, they were caught, tortured and even killed."

"Yes, you are right."

His fat wife said as she approached us while I did not noticed.

"And some of the Japanese soldiers were vicious. They robbed many rings and watches from the local residents and proudly showed it off. This is one of the reasons why I hate to go to the Philippines. How can I dare to go there for a memorial service after we committed? Although one of them proudly showed off a golden watch which he had stolen from the house of a dentist, he has already gone to the Philippines four or five times. I cannot understand why he can go there to attend a memorial service while forgetting what he had done in the past. They are perhaps going to the Philippines just for sight-seeing, if they go now. I heard they played with women during their last night in Manila.

I have never gone there for a memorial service. I hate to go. I could not feel secured because I could not relate sincerely with the locals. I could not feel at ease, when our unit entered a village and when I went out as a courier I could not walk calmly. I hate Filipino because their level was low and they have bad hygiene."

And his wife said.

"I also oppose my husband going to the Philippines. I heard a former soldier from North Area in Japan had gone there for a memorial service and he was told by the villagers, 'You must be the soldier who was stationed in this village during the war.' They said that he had been scared because the villagers had surrounded him."

"Do you ask me if I have a wish to apologize to Filipinos? No, I don't have. Rather, we had a lot of awful experiences."

"What I learned from my experience in the war? I hate militarism. I hated being a soldier, too. I did not like a war wherein you have to kill people, too. But through that experience, I learned to live by using my brain, bearing with hardships and deficiency."

When I went out to the main road, I saw many policemen. I thought they were on red alert for a demonstration against imperial coronation ceremony which be held in four days' time.

For what purpose are you asking this to me?

Yamada-san drove me in his car to the house of Kinji Yamamoto.

When I opened the glass door, I saw an old woman in the living room she drinking tea with her shoulders hunched.

Though Yamamoto-san was almost seventy years old, he has no white hair; his white heavy-jowled face was smooth and spotless.

"I heard you planted bombs when ordered by your Squad Leader Sasaki in the 'guerrilla subjugation' of Bauan.

Because I was told by one of my acquaintances about his role as a bomb expert during the subjugation of Bauan, I questioned him at once without wasting time.

At the moment, he smiled an embarrassed look, but he started talking about irrelevant topics.

"I was a first class private when we were in the outskirts of Mt. Macorodo. One day I attacked an encampment of U.S. Forces as a leader of our group. Though we managed to approach the encampment of the Americans, bomb exploded a 10 kg bomb. But we mishandled it, it exploded prematurely U.S. Forces, noticed us. We retreated with difficulty and approached U.S. Forces again around 3 o'clock in the morning. We succeeded in blowing them up while they were resting. By the success of our effort, our unit was not completely destroyed. Our commander thanked me."

He talked rapidly, feathing at the mouth. Then, he talked eagerly about how he was wounded on his shoulder and how one of his comrades was killed, his thigh cut off by a fragment of a bomb shell.

"I want to go back to the incident in Bauan. What kind of explosive did you use? ... I heard you used dynamites."

"No, they weren't dynamites. They were yellow explosives in canvas bags. I prepared four of them by putting firing devices on them.

"I heard you shot the wounded residents who came out of their houses with machine gun right after the blast.

"No, we used bayonets. Why do you ask? For what purpose?" he replied. I saw his head and neck became red a little."

I explained the purpose of my research again.

"We did not conduct subjugation out of our own free will. We had to do it because we were ordered. Unfortunately, we were the ones ordered. Who in earth would want that? We obeyed the order believing it was for our nation. Our former detail leader asked us to forget what happened in the war and to keep quiet. We decided we must not tell the truth. But I cannot forget. The miserable feelings linked to that subjugation has stayed in the hearts of those who had conducted the massacre and we cannot just forget it. It still smoulders in my heart. I can never tell it even to my wife and children. Never."

"In Bauan, Batangas, the guerrillas were so active that you killed all the males in the town."

"I didn't know but I just followed the order."

"From the viewpoint of Filipinos, it was just a war between U.S. and Japan, but their land became a battlefield. Their food was commandeered and their fields were destroyed. Moreover, many of them were massacred while undergoing subjugation. And Japan did not pay even a peso to the war victims in the Philippines after the war. Is it all right?" I asked him.

"Well, even though we had given them some compensation, they cannot mend their wounded hearts. I want to apologize, too," Yamamoto-san agreed. "But we got a bad deal. The elder soldiers punched us when we were fresh recruits. We had to obey their orders even though we hate to do so. And now I am not receiving a pension because the length of my service was short only for one year." (To receive a pension, a Japanese veteran should have rendered 15 years of military service).

"In Bauan, there are survivors of the massacre who were wounded in the explosion. What do you want to say to those victims in case you meet them?" I asked.

"I pity them. We are responsible for their bitter experience, but our apology won't change anything."

The Emperor's Order

I rode on a privately run trainway for twenty minutes and got off at a small station. I visited Goro Sasaki, leader of an engineering squad responsible for setting the yellow explosives in the subjugation of Bauan."

"The Japanese Imperial Army began conducting 'guerrilla subjugation' in the villages around Taal Lake in the middle of February 1945. It went on until the end of that month. Did you participate in these operations?" I asked.

"Yes, I did," he said. His shoulders were held low when he answered me in a weak voice.

"What did the technical squad do during the subjugation of Taal?"

"We did just what an infantry had to do," he said.

"Filipinos testified that the Japanese Imperial Army used yellow explosives to death 348 people in Bauan. I assume that the technical squad had prepared the explosives. Sasaki-san, were you there?"

He was silent and looked down.

"Were you there?" I again asked.

He nodded slightly.

"The order by the corps commander did not specify the method of subjugation. Who planned the use of explosives." I continued.

"I don't know. I think it was the battalion or company commander, but I am not sure."

"Why did you try to kill all the males in the town?"

"It was because of guerrillas. Guerrillas were responsible for it. The guerrillas ambushed Japanese soldiers in valleys when they went out for procuring food. Among fourteen or fifteen soldiers, all were killed except for only two persons. The guerrillas had a supply of weapon from America for their activities. Even children and women had hand grenades. One of our soldiers was cut on his neck when he entered a private house to ask for some water to drink."

"Did you see it?"

"No, I just heard of it."

"Sasaki-san, what will you do if the Philippine Army invaded Japan and does what the Japanese Army did in the Philippines?

"Well... "

He made a sound on his throat as if he was suffering.

"Was there any special reason to kill even women and children in the subjugation of Taal?"

"It was a cruel operation, when we think about it now. But we were not in a normal mindset then. It may be called as the battlefield psychology. Also, we were young, audacious, and bullheaded. We are still alive today, but we didn't know if we would be still alive tomorrow. Naturally, we became abnormal. We could not be same enough to know what we were really doing. Because if we mere same, we could not even harm a baby.

And even though we had a doubt on harsh and cruel orders, we were not permitted to resist them because in those times the order given by our senior officer was considered the order of the Emperor. Soldiers like us had to obey any order issued by our senior officer, however unreasonable it is.

"Now, I am seventy years old. When I think about my days the army, the military education completely neglected the individuality and humanity of soldiers.

But, it's impossible to listen each soldier's opinion and modify an order."

We must not start a war any more. I hope our homeland will not become a battlefield."

The Officer's Alibi

Masaru Tagawa agreed to meet me in the station of, a privately in the suburb of a big city. He was the commander when Taal and Bauan were subjugated.

He was a big and fat man. And came to me with his shoulders down and sporting a somewhat depressed look.

We sat down by a window at a small table in a coffee shop while facing each other.

"Of course, you know about what happened in Taal and Bauan, don't you? Your unit conducted a guerrilla subjugation or so-called massacre of residents there," I said.

"It might have happened in Bauan. But I doubt if it took place in Taal, too," he replied. "I was lying on the slopes of Mt. Macolod hut all by myself because I was sick. The night before, I was invited to a dance in a village. I had to drink some water."

"Is it justifiable to implement "uninhabitable operation" in Taal and Bauan, when look back on them now?

"Of course, it was justifiable. It was because the guerrillas disturbed the operations of the Japanese Imperial Army."

"Do you mean to say the Japanese Imperial Army had invaded the Philippines in the first place?" I asked.

"Did you say we invaded?" His eyes suddenly flashed with some recognition.

"Filipinos invited the Japanese Imperial Army?" I asked.

"No, they didn't, but..." he answered.

"If the Japanese invaded the Philippines with arms, don't you think naturally there will be guerrilla activities against them?" I asked.

"I am not sure," he said.

"The Japanese Imperial Army killed women and children. They killed men indiscriminately, assuming them as guerrillas. Even with this fact, do you think the order was right?"

"It is unbelievable. Because I thought it is not right to kill the person in the other country without proper reasons, I cannot believe that those soldiers I have trained did such cruel acts."

"But, Tagawa-san, those former soldiers under your directions clearly testified that the order for subjugation was issued to kill even women and children."

"I can't believe that my unit was involved. During that time, the Japanese Imperial Army was preparing for the expected landing of U.S. Forces in Batangas. So, the commando called as 'Gyorotai' which makes suicide attacks against warships and other base battalions were there. It was possible that other units committed the massacre."

"Do you mean to say that your unit did not conduct the subjugation of Taal subjugation?"

"I have no memory of it," he said.

"Don't you really remember? I cannot believe it. Lt. Matsuno was executed for being responsible for both incidents. He was one of your men and worked as an assistant for the aide-de-camp in the battalion headquarters. He testified in the military court that you had given him the order for subjugation."

"It was a mere tactic in the court. He said so because I had been sick when the subjugation happened..."

"It is strange, Matsuno-san testified that you recovered from illness before they conducted the operations in Taal and Bauan."

"No, I didn't," he replied.

When I read Matsuno-san's testimony, he comes to me as a splendid person for he did not deny his responsibility for conducting both subjugations.

"It is up to you how you appreciate him, but I was sick at that time."

"Japanese massacred many innocent Filipinos in the subjugation. Do you wish to apologize to them?" I asked.

"No, I don't wish to. It was a war, there must be killing. But ordinary citizens would never roam in the battlefield. So, I cannot believe those claims that innocent residents were killed or that women and children were killed. Let me say it again, I believe those soldiers I have trained did not conduct such evil act."

"The residents did not roam around in the battlefield. But the unit under Tagawa-san attacked the people in the villages of Taal."

"You may be wrong, I think," he said while facing in the other direction.

PLEASE EXTEND THE COMPENSATION FOR THE LIVES LOST

The Emperor was in the highest position in Japan, wasn't he?

Though it was not very far from the municipal hall of Taal to the town of Lemery, I got on a jeepney. The jewelry shop where Mrs. Amelia Montenegro was working was located in the crowded town where tricycles ran around with loud noise.

"Do you went to about the war victims? My mother, my grandmother, my aunt, and me. I was the only survivor. I was only eight month old then."

She wore a make-up on her fatty round face and put on eye shadow on her eyes.

"Because I was only a baby, I didn't remember anything, but when I was in the elementary school, I was told what had happened during the war.

We evacuated to Barangay Maput on the shore of Lake Taal to settle with the Castillos, a Spanish family. Because my mother was working for that family, the Japanese army massacred us together with them.

My another aunt told this. Because Japanese army attacked, we escaped into a tunnel-like place near the lake. After a while, my grandmother went out from the tunnel to look for water. But she was found and shot by a Japanese soldier. As my mother saw it and went out to rescue my grandmother, my mother was stabbed with bayonet, too. Then, the Japanese soldiers entered the tunnel and started killing the members of Castillo family. 7 of us were killed and three children survived. A one-month-old baby also survived.

When my mother was killed, she held me in her arm. So, I was stabbed on my left leg with bayonet. But they said I held on to my mother sucking her breast. A man in the village passed by there and saved me. He brought me to a small house where he evacuated. But when he noticed the Japanese army were around, he ran away to somewhere leaving the chopped sugar cane and a cup of water for me. It was maybe because I cried out. A childless couple passed by there and they brought me along with them. Later on, my father and my aunt found me and asked them to return me. But I heard that they refused to return me. But anyway, I was returned at last. Then, I was brought to a hospital managed by Americans for the treatment of my leg. Since I became big enough, I have been so afraid of Japanese. Though there was no Japanese anymore, I was so scared and ran away when I saw a Filipino soldier uniformed carrying gun."

"Did Japanese try to kill everybody because they could distinguish who was a guerrilla and who wasn't? It is terrible. It is only the selfish idea of those killers.

This is an experience of my father. Because my house was near the barrack of the Japanese army, the Japanese soldiers often visited there. I heard that my parents have several friends with Japanese. My father said some of them had brought food and others had shed tears when they listened to a tune of piano from a house in our neighbor. He also said some Japanese soldiers had said he did not want to join the army but he was forced to do. But my family was massacred in the evacuation site. Even though some of Japanese were kind enough to bring blankets for us."

"Do you ask me about my opinion who was responsible for the resident massacre in Taal? I think the responsibility must be with the Japanese government in those times. I think the Emperor is especially responsible, though the direct responsibility for the killing of my mother and grandmother was with the officer who ordered it."

"Why is the Emperor responsible? It is because he was in the highest position in Japan. I believe there had not been Taal massacre if the Emperor did not order to kill even the residents."

I will never forgive as long as I live.

I went to Barangay Luntal from the town of Taal by tricycle because there was no jeepney for this route.

It was hot, the sun was strong of the road dusty. I was the first Japanese who visited this barangay after the end of the war.

Because the barangay captain was absent, his elder brother guided me to the house of the war victims. While we were walking, he started to talk to me as if he was mumbling.

"One week before the Japanese army attacked the barrio, the Japanese Imperial Army came to the village and took away two cows, one carabao and all the fowls. They brought them without paying any military currency. Though we wanted to complain, we just had to be patient and quiet because the soldiers had guns," he said.

Perhaps upon hearing his words, the other old man approached me and said as if talking to himself.

"They also took one cow from my house. Can you negotiate compensation for it?"

Mrs. Solidad Tersona was almost killed with a bayonet when she was nineteen years old. When she fell down, she was stabbed strongly on her left armpit with bayonet and it penetrated her lung out to the right side.

She observed me cautiously and sat on the end of the long wooden bench on which I sat down so that she could be away from me as much as possible.

"Though I only have one deep wound, there were also small wounds on my arm, perhaps because he tried to stab me several times. My nerve in the right arm seemed to be cut and I could not move it well."

She said in a faint voice.

"On that day, we evacuated from the barrio to the mountain. In the early next morning, I returned to the barrio with my uncle, aunt and cousins to check the situation. In the early morning of the day, we saw smoke coming up and it seemed our house was set on fire. We never thought the Japanese soldiers were still hiding but then they suddenly attacked us and stabbed us with bayonets. All of them were killed only I was the one who survived. The Japanese soldiers thought I was dead with the terrible wound. Though they kicked the bodies with their feet to check if we were really dead. I wasn't kicked because there was another body beside me.

Three days after, my neighbors found I was still alive when they passed by me though I looked like a dead body. They noticed I was groaning and immediately dressed my wound by cutting a piece of clothe from my dress. Though they brought me to a sugar factory, they left me there because they were afraid the Japanese would come again. In the night of that day, two or three neighbors came and brought me to a Filipino doctor in Tagaytay. I was brought there on a hammock because my condition was serious. But I was brought back to the barrio just after one day stay with the doctor because the Japanese army would pass there. After I stayed for one day, we had to move because Japanese would pass again. But because the Japanese army appeared so suddenly, the men in the village run away and left me. Fortunately, the Japanese army just passed by and did nothing. When the men came back, they said we would be safer in Tagaytay. So, we went there. In Tagaytay, we heard U.S. Forces was in Taal. So we went Taal. There were a lot of people who had escaped from various places for the fear of Japanese army. I was admitted to the hospital operated by U.S. Forces and treated for about ten weeks. So, I managed to recover.

During that time, an American army surgeon said to me, 'I am glad because you survive even though your condition was very serious.' Later on, my uncle made an arrangement for me so that I would be treated in a hospital in Laguna province managed by U.S. Forces. It took one year and a half before my wound healed completely. Even now my left breast aches from time to time because I was stabbed on it.

I got married after the liberation and had five children. I am now living a simple but happy life.

I still hate the Japanese. I hate especially the Japanese who tried to kill me with bayonet. This interview is also a rather unpleasant experience for me. Because this reminds me the terrible experience in the past."

"Do you ask me what I want to say to those surviving Japanese soldiers? I want to shout at them to the top of my voice until my lungs will be cleared."

Her neighbors who were listening laughed to what she said.

"Is it true? The reason why they tried to kill us was to wipe guerrillas out? . . . if they still believe that I will never forgive the Japanese who tried to kill me. I also don't forgive the members of his unit. I will never forgive them as long as I live. From time to time when my wound on the chest aches, it pains me to recall the cruel massacre.

We cannot tell what they will do to us again

An old woman wearing an old sky-blue one-piece dress was standing in the living room of the house of Mrs. Tersona, we did not notice when she came in. She stood in front of me and turned her back to me and suddenly rolled up the skirt of her dress up to her back.

"Look at it. Look at my body."

I found there was a scar of old burn spread from her back to her right thigh, when I looked at her back thoroughly.

She was Mrs. Maria Banawa. The Japanese Imperial Army killed her husband and two of her brothers.

"We built a small house and evacuated in the house in a place a little bit away from the barangay because we were afraid of the Japanese army. On that day, when I was preparing breakfast, the Japanese soldiers came with gun attached with bayonet. Because I thought they would kill us, I knelt down and implored desperately to him as if I was praying to God, "Please don't kill me." But he stabbed me with his bayonet and I fell down to the ground. He set fire on my skirt and also on my house. I lost consciousness outside of the house, but I came to consciousness in the afternoon. The fire set on my skirt spread and I suffered burn injury even on my back. My cousin and neighbors found me when they passed by. And they put me on the back of a horse and brought me to a safe mountain. They treated my wounds with mixed coconut oil and mustard. But it hurt me a lot and I cried out every time they put the medicine.

Like Tersona, I fled away to Taal and other various places as we were told the Japanese Imperial Army would pass by. And then I was treated in a field hospital by U.S. Forces in Lemery. It took more than nine years before my wound completely healed.

I was pregnant and had to give birth to my baby then. But because my wound on the back was not healed, I gave birth to my eldest daughter in a terribly awkward position."

As she said it with gestures, the women listening to our conversation laughed in lower voice.

"I was a widow even before giving birth to my child. I cried out because my back ached while giving birth to her.

She looked at her daughter standing at the entrance.

"About my remarriage? Well, seven years after my husband was killed, a man said to me he wanted to marry me. So, we got married."

The women around us laughed again.

*Mrs. Solidad Tersona, Maria Banawa and
her daughter (from right to left).*

"I am still angry with the Japanese. I can never forgive them. I am angry especially with the soldier who set fire on my skirt. If I meet that Japanese, I will be scared while I get angry with him. It is because I cannot tell what he will do to me again. I want to slap a Japanese with all my strength even only once."

The women around us laughed again.

"Do you ask me whether I have anything to say to those surviving Japanese soldiers? Yes, I have. Why did they massacre our family? What wrong have we done to the Japanese army? Even I knelt down and implored as if I prayed to the God saying, 'Please don't kill us. Please don't set fire,' they didn't listen to me. I want to ask them the reason. And I want them to apologize."

"Do you want to know whether I can forgive the Japanese Army if they come here to apologize? ... I am scared. Even if the Japanese come here to apologize to me, I am afraid to meet with them. They might hide another bayonet. I am afraid and I cannot trust Japanese.

When I heard a Japanese is coming to this barangay, I was surprised and my heart ached.

But are you really a Japanese?"

She looked into my face.

"This is because I cannot believe you are Japanese. You do not have a gun and a pistol."

I focused my tape recorder to her daughter standing in the entrance.

"What I want to tell Japanese? . . . listening to what my mother said, I felt pain and sorrow. When I was born, I didn't have a father. Though my mother remarried, it was very hard for me to live with a stepfather. I wished many times that my father is alive. Why did the Japanese kill my father?"

She shed tears and her lips trembled.

They left only hatred in the heart of Filipinos

I went to the town of Bauan. In this town the Japanese army gathered the male residents to church in the name of "guerrilla subjugation" and blasted them after confining them in the house of Mr. Bautista, a wealthy citizen in the town.

When I pushed the door of the office of the town mayor, Mayor Castillio looked up to me. He had white hair and a big body. Because it was the second time for him to see me, he allowed me to interview him at once.

"Because the war was a part of the history, I don't have any complaints to Japanese anymore. And Japan is assisting and investing in the Philippines now.

But I still remember my father from time to time. He was brought to an elementary school, used as an internment camp by Japanese Imperial Army. Then, he disappeared four days after and he had not returned until now. I could not know where he had been killed or I tried to confirm if he had been brought to Cuenca, but I couldn't. Because he had a weak leg, he could have not gone that far."

"The strategy of the Japanese Imperial Army was totally wrong. They blasted the residents to death to wipe the guerrillas out but the guerrillas in Bauan, could have not attacked the Japanese army because they didn't have any weapon. I was one of the leaders of ROTC Guerrilla (A guerrilla group composed of former students who have been trained in a military course in college.) During that time, only the guerrilla group in Bolo Island in Lake Taal had weapon in this area."

"The blasting operation by the Japanese Imperial Army was absurd. They tried to wipe out all men by bombing and they burned almost all houses in the town by pouring gasoline, but those operations only resulted adverse effects. They left only hatred in our hearts."

"Do you ask me whether I will forgive those Japanese who were involved in the blasting incident, if they come here to apologize? Of course I will forgive them. I will welcome and invite them to this office. And I will even hold a welcome party."

Last year, I went to Japan. The Japanese now are totally different from those Japanese in the past. Though the Japanese army became cruel in the end of the war, it was because of the war. If the Philippine army had invaded and occupied Japan, they might have made more cruel acts. They might have tortured, massacred and ran after the women. Because the soldiers in the Philippines are not educated well, the result might have been much worse. We should blame the war, because a war makes men crazy."

"Do you say I am generous, even though my father was killed? Thank you. . . . But I am human, too. I also happened to think of my father sometimes. I tried to find the body of my father by digging up the surroundings of the elementary school used as an internment camp by Japanese army but it was all in vain. My father will never return from his tomb."

*The church where the residents of
Bauan were brought.*

The responsibility for massacres? Koreans massacred us, didn't they?

Mr. Teodorico Gonzales was very thin and sat in the entrance of his house with his shoulders down. Four sewing machines were roaring and a baby continued crying in the room.

"One morning, I woke up because somebody was shouting loudly. We were gathered by the Japanese soldiers and brought to the church. And then we were brought to the house of Mr. Bautista."

He said in loud voice as if to compete against the noise from the sewing machines.

"In the moment when the surrounding became dark, it got bright suddenly as if it was daytime. I tried to run away. But because there were Japanese soldiers in the direction of the church, I jumped out from the broken window in the other side. The Japanese soldiers shot at me at once. But I couldn't understand what happened then, though I heard the sound of shooting. When I managed to escape and got relaxed, I noticed blood spurting out from the upper part of my right chest. I was shot from my chest and the bullet penetrated out through my back.

I escaped to Barangay San Antonio and my uncle helped me there. He treated me with the mixture of coconut oil and mustard until my wound healed. One month after when U.S. Forces arrived, they brought me to a field hospital in Muntinlupa, I was admitted there and survived. But I wonder what would have happened to me if I was not treated there."

"I heard Japan is now industrialized and developed. Perhaps Japanese now are not cruel like in the past except those Yakuzas.

Why did they try to kill us though we were innocent? Do you say they blasted men to wipe the guerrillas out? For Christ's sake, it is a selfish reasoning."

"The responsibility for trying to massacre us? Weren't they Koreans? I heard they used to be more cruel than Japanese."

"Do you want to know how we could recognize the difference between Japanese and Korean? It was easy because Korean wore shoes that had split toes. Did Japanese also wear such shoes? And we couldn't tell which is which? Is it true?'

A small woman in her 60's started talking though I did not know when she came here.

"I had a Japanese friend during that time. And we were very close friends. His name was Watanabe or Tanaka. So I could tell the difference between Korean and Japanese. The skin of Korean was darker than that of Japanese."

"Is it true that even Japanese cannot tell the difference between Korean and Japanese by the color of their skin? Is it true? . . . I believed it because the soldier had told me."

The small woman said in an unconvinced look.

"Everybody believe's so."

Mr. Gonzales said.

Can they understand the pain in my heart?

Mr. Geronimo Madlambayan lost his eye sight at the age of sixteen in that blast. Coming up the stone stairs by a few steps in his frail foot falls with his niece in his arm, he returned to the living room. He noticed my visit by hearing my footsteps.

When I and Francisco, my interpreter, were requested to sit down. Mr. Madlambayan took a seat, leaned forward and started talking in clear English.

"Captain Matsuno came from Cuenca to Bauan and brought all the male residents to the house of Mr. Bautista to be bombed.

Though I was blinded suddenly, my brother-in-law saved me. Because the Japanese were killing the surviving residents and set the town on fire, we escaped to Barangay Dambulayan after observing the situation. It was a quiet village near the sea."

When I looked at his face closely, I noticed there was a wound under his left eye. He said there are also several wounds on his chest.

"Then, I was treated for two weeks in a field hospital managed by U.S. Forces. But after the Americans moved to Lipa, they did not treat me anymore.

"Can the Japanese understand this pain in my heart? I was still in my prime. But I was thrown into a world of darkness. The wounds not only on my body but also in my heart have not yet healed. I hated the Japanese very deeply because they disabled me."

"Twelve years ago, a Japanese engineer came here to work. He and I became friends. My feeling toward the Japanese has changed somehow," he revealed.

"Do you know that some of those Japanese soldiers are still alive?" I said.

"Is that so? Please tell those Japanese that I want them to help me. I am poor and living a hard life since I became blind," he said.

"What's your job since you became blind?" I inquired quite inconsiderately.

"How could I work? I have managed only through the kindness of my brothers and relatives," he said.

"Are you married?" I asked.

"Do you think I could get married and have a family even though I have no work?" he retorted.

Juanito Arbal: Trust Betrayed

Juanito Arbal was so thin one might be inclined to exaggerate that only bones covered with skin make up his body. When I went to his house to interview him, I saw Mr. Madlang-bayan staying with him.

"What was your unforgettable war experience?" I asked Juanito.

"The blast. On the day it happened, I was working for the Japanese Army as a policeman. The male residents had been herded in the church. Then I made them stand in line and had them brought to Mr. Bautista's house. I entered that house with the others. I do not want to enter it but I was forced to do so by the Japanese soldiers.

" 'You must enter, too,' they said. Because I like them, I cooperated with them. So I could not understand why they tried to kill me," he complained.

"What do you want me to tell those Japanese soldiers who are still alive?" I asked.

The house of Mr. Bautista was located around this area.

"Well, I want to thank tem. They took care of me when I was working for them," he said.

"Were those killed by the Japanese soldiers civilians or guerrillas?" I asked.

"They were ordinary people. Almost all of them," he revealed.

"Why did you cooperate with the Japanese soldiers?" I asked.

He explained: "As a policeman at the time, my duty was mainly to look for guerrillas. I trusted the Japanese then. That's why I cooperated with them, but . . .", he said in a faint voice.

Pedro Alaño: A Wish for Revenge

Pedro Alaño is huge, fat and has a triple chin. In his cool front garden here were mahjong tables under the trees; it was encircled with metal mesh fence. There were two groups of people playing mahjong.

During the war in his dark living room, I listened to his story.

"My father and three of my uncles were killed in that explosion. I was fifteen and narrowly escape death. That early morning before going to church, my father gave me a sack it contains rings, necklaces, bracelets, and other valuables. He told me, his eldest son, "You must take these with you at all cost; these are precious items I've made. He is a jewel craftsman as well. My father owns land in his hometown and he told me to go in a hurry, that I must hide in the barrio as he noticed the activities of the Japanese Army becoming cruel. Before I left, I helped him in bringing rice to a bomb shelter. I had to evacuate with my mother, but since I am a curious young boy, I went to the church were the villagers were herded without telling her.

"I sat with them. I saw a mother and her daughter crying. They are from Leyte. 'What brings you here?' I asked. The mother said they came here to look for her son, a soldier in the USAFFE (U.S. Armed Forces in the Far East) that saw action in Bataan.

Then, women and children had to go out, leaving the men inside. They tried hard to persuade me to come with them. 'Please come with us, we don't know anyone; we don't have any food,' they said. But I declined their request by saying that my body was big for my age and the Japanese soldiers would not consider me as a boy. But the mother offered the clothes of her daughter to me and disguising myself as a girl, We hurriedly went out from that church. So I luckily save myself.

"Life was very hard since my father was killed. I had three sisters and seven brothers in my family. My eldest sister was seventeen years old and my youngest sibling was two. Because I was the eldest, I quit school and started farming. I grew vegetables and sold them in the town. It was a hard life."

"If my father was not killed, I might have graduated from college and become a professional. If only that explosion did not take place. "But why did the Japanese Army try to kill all the men in this town?" he asked.

"Do you know that they plotted to kill all the men in your town to wipe out the guerrillas?" "It is a terrible reasoning. There was no guerrilla activity in this town. My father was not a guerrilla, he continued; From the point of view of the Japanese Army, everybody looks like a guerrilla?" he asked." "Perhaps it came as a result of our distrust of the Japanese Army and they also did not trust us Filipinos. But that was a treacherous act. I was so afraid of the Japanese but I was a boy and I wanted to take revenge," he said.

"Who do you think is responsible for the blast?" I asked.

"The officer who gave the order is most responsible. But the individual soldiers who tried to kill us are also responsible. One day a Japanese soldier stopped me. "Kora!" ("Halt!") he said. 'Are you a guerrilla?' he asked. The moment I answered, 'No I am not,' he slapped me. And the soldier who knows me took the sack of valuables I was carrying. I am sure his senior officer did not order him to do so but he did it on his own. So this soldier must be held responsible for his acts. The Japanese always blame orders and their senior officer, that is cowardly," he said. His big fat belly jerked.

"Are you still angry at the Japanese?" I asked him. "Yes of course I am still angry," he said.

"If those Japanese who were involved in the massacre of residents in Bauan will come to visit here and apologize, can you forgive them?" I asked. "I don't know. It is easy to say in words, I can 'forgive' if they apologize, but I am not sure if I can forgive them sincerely. On the other hand, I still have a wish to take revenge. I cannot make up my mind right now," he said.

One of the men playing mahjong shouted, he had been shouting at me to catch my attention. He again asked, "Why did the Japanese kill Filipinos though their enemy is America? I want to know why."

Not a peso for Simon Adap's pain and suffering

Simon Adap was short and had a shop in a market. The width of his shop was three meters and he was selling general merchandise there.

When I introduced myself and my purpose of investigating at Japanese war crimes, he took off his shirt suddenly to bare the upper half of his body to show me his scars inflicted by a bayonet. There were three scars around his nipples and one near his spinal column. He said he has another scar on his hip, and pointed at it.

"Then we were transferred to Mr. Bautista's house. Inside I saw big objects hanging from the ceiling. Soon the Japanese soldiers closed the door. A loud explosion! We fell down. But I was not wounded . . . So, I jumped out from a broken window. But the soldiers were waiting for us and I was stabbed three times in my chest and also on my back and hip."

He opened both of his eyes so widely that one might be afraid if his eyes would pop out. And he continued his story with bulging eyes staring at me.

"Then, I lost consciousness and fell down on the road. When I gained consciousness, I noticed that the houses in the town are burning. Because then the Japanese soldiers came back and they started to hunt for survivors, I pretended to be dead. The Japanese soldiers searched everywhere.

Because my condition was serious, I remained lying on the road. I could not even stand up to look for something to drink and eat. Though I was still breathing, I could do nothing, because I was almost killed. I have a wife and two children. She was out looking for my body when the Japanese soldiers had gone. She found me crawling on the ground. Then, for two weeks she applied a mixture of coconut oil and mustard on me. But because my condition did not improve, I was sent to an American field hospital when the Americans reached our place. During that time, I was angry at the Japanese. I have been thinking of taking revenge when I have fully recovered. This feeling still remains. However, right after the Liberation, the mayor of Bauan said that the massacre was perpetrated by Koreans.

"No, you completely misunderstand. The officers and the one who caused the explosion were all Japanese," I clarified.

"Is it true? This is the first time for me to hear that," he said.

"Do you have anything to say to those Japanese who are still living," I asked. "Yes I have. Because it took 2 years before my wounds got healed, I want them to compensate me for my pain and suffering. Three wounds on my chest still caused me pain," he said.

"Have you received any compensation from the Philippine government?" I asked. "No not a single cent. So I had to demand compensation from the Japanese. Don't you think it is but right and proper for me to ask this since they almost killed me?" he asked.

In Japan I tried to find out how Japan's war reparations to the Philippines had been used. From 1956 to 1976, Japan paid U.S. $550 million of reparation to the Philippines in the period of twenty years. For my astonishment, not a centavo was given to the war victims in the Philippines, though I once believed that the reparation from 1956 to 1976 had already been paid using our tax money and as way to apologize for Japan's having devastated the Philippines during the war.

Ninoy Aquino, revealed the following in an interview he had with a reporter of Sankei Publishing Bureau.

Thirty percent of the reparations from Japan [which is in cash] was used to fund government projects. The rest or 70% of it was distributed in kind to private companies: ship, shipbuilding, cement, and textile. These industrial products and labor were acquired by the Filipino companies at very cheap prices. Likewise, Japanese companies earned big profits from this transaction. As a result, these corrupted Filipinos. For example, Company [Japanese] M, which was close to President Marcos, sold a fertilizer factory to a Filipino company as Japan's reparations valued at U.S. $90 million actually cost about U.S. $75 million. President Marcos and his cronies got the U.S. $15 million as kickback (rebate) by brokering this transaction. ("The True Faces of Neighbors: In the Gap of Compensation and Assistance")

Simon Adap (left), a survivor of the Bauan explosion

Chapter 5

Aftermath of the Battlefields

I have traveled to various parts of Japan from Tohoku to Kita-Kyushu and I have interviewed a hundred officers and men who served in the Japanese Imperial Army. And I came notice that there are two remaining problems.

One of them is that those who were tried in the War Tribunal in the Philippines after the war have been severely criticizing it. "That trial was completely wrong. They wanted to execute anyone as long as he is a Japanese. But we cannot consider this if we exclude the fact that these soldiers killed. Japanese Army implemented indiscriminately mass massacre many Filipinos residents in the name of 'guerrilla subjugation' in Laguna and Batangas provinces as I mentioned in earlier chapter of this book.

How do Filipino think and answer to this accusation by the former Japanese soldiers and officers?

And another problem is the memorial services carried out by the Japanese. The veterans' group called The Philippine Islands Group of 17th Infantry Regiment of Akita built Jizo and Goddess of Mercy statues in three places in both of Laguna and Batangas to comfort the spirit of their dead comrades, calling those statues as Japanese Maria. And also they visit the Philippines bringing a lot of souvenir items and hold Japanese-style ceremony including incense offering and ching reading every year.

And Japanese government built "The statue for the war victims in the Philippine islands" in Caliraya in the southern part of Luzon island during Marcos era. This Caliraya cemetery includes vast Japanese-style garden. It is also called as "Japanese Garden". Many of Japanese groups visit there while they hold memorial services in the Philippines.

But how do Filipino feel on the erections of war memorials and the visits for memorial service, while their land was made a battlefield and devastated, they were wounded and even lost their parents?"

I visited Japanese and Filipinos further to ask those questions.

Saburo Sekiguchi: A War Criminal

Saburo Sekiguchi sits at a kotatsu (a table with a heater) in a four-tatami room. He welcomed me with a dismal and gloomy look.

"Is it true you were tried as a war criminal?" I asked.

"I was only a first class private, and yet I was convicted as a war criminal," he said.

He was charge as a war criminal for conducting subjugation in Barrio Lumban in Lipa. During that time, Americans were closing in on Laguna and Batangas.

Although he was severely injured by the attacked of the guerrillas, an American army surgeon saved him. He stayed for a half year in a hospital operated by American doctors in Manila and survived.

"What happened?"

"After I recovered, I was brought to an interment camp in Canlubang. There I worked as a garbage collector by driving a truck. During that time, we were asked, Anybody here who is with the XX Airfield Battalion? I answered, "Me". We secured Lipa Airfield in Lipa City, Batangas and its surroundings. I was ordered to pack up. Then brought to Manila. The Americans put on trial in the War Tribunal," he said.

"Are you guilty?" I asked.

"No, I'm not, I was just a witness of the massacre by the Japanese Army from the other side of a river or on the bank of river, I was prosecuted in the War Tribunal. Those soldiers who participated in the subjugation used false names and they did not admit they were stationed in Lipa. And some of them even returned to Japan," he said.

"Why didn't you also use false name like them to save yourself?" I asked.

"But I could not know or do so because I had just returned from the hospital. That's why I honestly admitted I belonged to the XX Airfield Battalion," he said.

"But they said it was a fair trial," I said.

"It wasn't. They really made a fool out of me. When Filipinos looked for suspects, they always point to me even though I did nothing wrong. That's how I became a war criminal. It's true there was a massacre of residents. But it was totally unfair that I was the one sentenced as guilty, my trial lasted for four years. And when the verdict came, they found me guilty. I was given a death sentence. Executions were held once or twice a week. The day before an execution, Filipinos were proudly talking with each other on how many holes they had dug. The following day, an officer came to our cellblock quietly to summon one of us. I wondered whether he would stop in front of my cell. If he stopped, it means I would die. If he passed me by, I would be relieved knowing that I will survive today. So many times I have experienced this feeling," he said.

"By the way, who was responsible for the guerrilla subjugation in Lumban?" I asked.

"It was the battalion commander, but he was killed during the war. There were also other commanders in the field, but they fled perhaps everyone wants to survive. But my life was ruined completely because I was convicted as a war criminal. But when I recall the past I think the Japanese Army was cruel. They treated the women, children and even old men harshly. Everytime they find girls in her 18 or 19 yr. old during subjugation, they take these girls with them and confine them in a comfort station. Moreover, when U.S. Liberation Forces were fast approaching, the Japanese Army decided they have no need to keep these young women anymore, so they threw them down alive into a well. Then threw stones at them and poured soil down into the well to kill them. But a girl manage to survive.

"How come you were not executed?" I asked.

"My sentence was reduced from death to life imprisonment. I was able to return to Japan in 1953. Just before (my release) I would come from the prison, because I was good at driving, I got a car license so that I could work. I passed it by taking an easy examination.

Then I worked in a transportation company for ten years. Before I resigned from the company, I have also joined and worked for a labor union. This was perhaps because I was rebellious against authority," he said.

"Did you participate in the peace movement after going through the experience in the war?"

"No I didn't. For some reason, I don't trust other people. I could not trust any people but myself," he said.

"By the way, I believe Japan cannot become a true democratic country as long as we keep this Emperor system. Think on the situation where one is shot with a pistol when he talks on the responsibility of the Emperor for the war like Mayor Motoshima in Nagasaki City. For example, you may want to criticize the fact that the government uses the tax money for the Emperor's coronation ceremony although the tax was collected from the people. But nobody cannot criticize it or talk on what he is thinking. I think this kind of atmosphere will intensify more and more in the future," he said shaking his head slightly.

"How could Japan change this atmosphere?" I asked.

"Maybe Japan had to be crushed again," said talking to himself.

Shiro Ohtani: War is Zaiaku (Evil)

I met Shiro Ohtani at his house. He was tried and found guilty for having participated in Bauan explosion. His back was a little bent. As soon as he sat on a chair, he started talking eagerly on how the War Tribunal in the Philippines had tried him unfairly.

"U.S. Forces did relatively correct trials. But after Philippines became independent and our trials were transferred to the Philippine side, the trials had become completely absurd and unfair and I was convicted with death penalty.

When I was confined in a jail as a war criminal, I wanted to tell the truth to my wife and children before I would die there. Executions were carried out every Friday. So, I tried to be saved spiritually by praying to God. But I wanted to clarify that I would be killed even though I was innocent. The reason I would be killed was that we were defeated in the war. Though I committed nothing wrong, I was made guilty forcibly for whatever I did not commit."

"You were the deputy commander of the XX Battalion of the XX Infantry Regiment at that time. Is it true that your battalion conducted the resident massacre in Bauan, didn't it?" I asked.

"Though I was the deputy commander, I was not in the position to issue orders," he answered.

By the way, the lawyers in U.S. Forces told us, 'A trial is a kind of game. You might achieve the judgment of not guilty if you testified smartly.' Based on their advice, we gave false testimonies on the location of our unit and other matters. And as a result, 8 were not sentenced with death penalty, although 9 were prosecuted. However, because the Filipinos hated the Japanese so deeply, they lied in their testimonies to make sure that all the Japanese soldiers charged in the War Tribunal are found or will be found guilty," he said.

"But Lt. Matsanu testified that "Taal subjugation" was mainly conducted by 150 soldiers and officers of the X Battalion, before he was executed. And was he not your assistant? He also testified that the same unit participated in the Bauan massacre." "Don't you think it is necessary you have to admit first that you killed hundreds of innocents in Taal and Bauan in the name of "guerrilla subjugation", before you claim that you were tried unfairly?" I asked.

"Those massacres might have happened but our trials were terribly unfair. Though most of the officers who were involved in those measures are now dead, the War Tribunal forcibly pinned us down as war criminals," he said.

"Why was it only Lt. Matsuno who was executed for the Bauan massacre? His role was merely to support you when you were a deputy in the battalion headquarters. He was not in command, wasn't he?" I asked.

"Matsuno speaks English and gets along with Bauan residents. To them, he is known as "Capt. Matsuno". As a result, they point him out as a perpetrator, making him guilty. "Why did no one try to save Lt. Matsuno, even though he was not directly involved?" I asked.

"We were busy to save ourselves and could not help others then," he answered.

"What can you think of the war now after 45 years?"

"War is evil. We must not make war. Many of my comrades were killed in that harsh battlefield. But the War Tribunal there was completely unfair. The most pitiful was the case of Capt. Chukichi Ito, a company commander. Though he was transferred to Los Baños during the "guerrilla subjugation" in Bai, he was executed for the responsibility of that incident. Capt. Yukio Suzuki, commander of the X Amphibious Battalion, ordered that subjugation. But Suzuki pretended he is crazy and was able to return to Japan, thus escaping from responsibility for the massacre. And Capt. Ito was unluckily made a victim in an unfair trial," he said.

"The problem worsened when those Japanese blamed others for their own faults. Before you complain about how the trial was conducted there, whatever happened to military spirit which respects courage and justice?"

"There was no such thing as justice in the Japanese Army in those times. I only thought of myself

214

because I want to save my life. The faith and justice, which once were taught us, were lost somewhere. But there was one respectable officer. He left a will for us. It said. 'When I die, eat my flesh so that you can survive,' while you are starving," he said.

"By the way, do you want to apologize to those Filipino war victims," I asked.

"Though we want to apologize, most of those responsible for Filipinos' misfortunes are now dead," he said.

"I'm not asking who is responsible for the massacre. Do you want to apologize to them – you, as an officer of the Japanese Army, and who devastated their country during the war?" I asked.

"Me as a Japanese who lived during that time, am I now ready to apologize? Why should I do that? I suffered a lot in that unfair trial," he concluded.

Goro Ohishi: Crossing the River to the After Life

A typhoon was hitting the Shizuoka area in central Japan, it was raining hard when I reached the house of Goro Ohishi located some five minutes away from a railway station run by a private corporation. He was a platoon leader in the Philippine battlefront.

"Who received the order from corps headquarters to conduct "guerrilla subjugation" in Taal and Bauan? Who gave the order to execute it?" I asked.

"Battalion Commander Tagawa is sick at the time. So Lt. Fujiki went to corps headquarters to receive the order. But Commander Tagawa gave that order to our unit," he said.

"I met with Tagawa-san. But when I asked him about it, he said he did not issue that order because he was then lying in bed due to dysentery," I said.

"Though he was ill, his condition was not so bad. So he surely gave the order," he said.

"After our defeat in Second World War, did the corps try to hide the fact that it had ordered the subjugation?"

"Yes it did. I heard that a general in the 14th area Army who was presented as a witness in the trial of General Yamashita was forbidden from revealing that fact. The corps told him: 'You must claim that their was no order for subjugation, for the honor of Japan.' As a result, the corps commander also denied the subjugation order. It caused an uproar among us because we assumed they would blame us, their subordinates for all the things they had committed. Later on, that corps commander changed his testimony and admitted his responsibility. He was hanged.

But because Battalion Commander Tagawa was a coward, he did not admit his fault. In the night before the verdict would be given to the war criminals, we severely blamed Tagawa because 9 of us had been persecuted. We said, 'Although you issued the order to subjugate guerrillas, you are claiming that you had been ill. If you avoid your responsibility, we will be punished, as we had been your subordinates.' We demanded him to testify the truth to midnight and he promised us to tell the truth in the court in the following day. But he broke his promise."

Goro Sasaki, who had been prosecuted for the Bauan explosion, also testified about Tagawa-san as follows:

"Because he believed that he would not meet us anymore when we would go back to Japan as he had been born in different area from us, he blamed his men from what he had committed by claiming that he not ordered. During that time even senior officers and comrades were blaming each other just to save themselves."

Now let us go back to the testimony by Mr. Ohishi.

"I was sentenced for twenty-five years of imprisonment and I served for ten years in Sugamo prison in Tokyo. I came out of prison when I was thirty-three years old. Though I wanted to work in my previous workplace, it wasn't possible because I was imprisoned for the charge of war crime.

Perhaps all those who were imprisoned in Sugamo believe this. We must not fight a war anymore. I thought strongly that people would suffer the same fate like us if war occurs.

– Do you think you had made or inflicted great sufferings to Filipinos?" I asked.

"Because it was war, we did anything just to win. So, the countries under the war suffered terribly and were greatly devastated. And since we started the war, all went wrong. So we must not wage that kind of war again," he said.

– Perhaps you do not visit the town of Bauan while it is the most necessary to apologize there. Though the town mayor says he welcome Japanese, many of the residents are still angry.

"I wish to apologize. But as we committed terrible cruelty in Bauan, it is difficult for us to visit there.

During that time, we put a cannon in the suburb of the town of Bauan. As black smoke rose up with a tremendous sound, we went there. We saw that a strong two-storey house was crashed down and burned bodies were piled up in the center of the house. People were lying around it unconscious. Those who managed to survive were killed by the soldiers. When I recall that scene, I cannot imagine going near that place because it was so terrible," he said.

– "Without doing anything, do you think those Japanese who committed such activities can cross the river leading to the afterlife?" I asked.

"On the other hand, I sometimes wonder if it is necessary to talk about it forty-five years after the war," he said.

"But don't you think there is a good opportunity now to achieve a reconciliation with the Japanese taking the initiative? Filipinos now can think about it calmly and Japanese are now beginning to think of apologizing."

"In my opinion, the coming years will be very important. Do we not want to cross the river leading to the afterlife – after we have built the road that will make up for those wrongdoings we have done during the war?"

"I believe that you are right, but . . .," he said and nodded a little.

The winds and the rain became more intense than before.

Seiji Sayama: "They should apologize, not me"

I went to the meeting place as instructed. I recalled his harsh way of speaking over the phone because he was reluctant to grant me an interview.

He was drinking coffee in the lounge, a coffee shop, when I arrived on the second floor of the meeting place. His hair is still black and his back is still straight inspite of his old age.

"I was convicted as a war criminal in 1946 and was able to return to Japan in 1954. Because I was rebellious, I joined the Self Defense Force when nobody wanted to join it. My friends told me, 'Do you want to be convicted again as a war criminal?'

Sayama-san became a high-ranking officer of the Self Defense Force.

– "The Japanese Army conducted "guerrilla subjugation" from February to March 1945. They look at them as military operations but the residents look at them as massacres. Is it true those "operations" were ordered by the corps commander on January 25?" I asked.

"I never heard of such an order," he said.

– "Is that so? But you are one of the generals of the corps. In fact you can find that order even in the 'War History Library 60, The Decisive Battle in Luzon issued by the Military History Department, The National Institute for Defense Studies, Japan Defense Agency, isn't it?

"What was written in that book is not accurate. Its contents were based merely on the hearings conducted with the colonels, who returned to Japan," he revealed.

Immediately however, he modified his statement:

"But in general that book is not wrong," he said.

"The Japanese Army massacred Filipinos in Laguna and Batangas in the name of "guerrilla subjugation." Were the guerrillas such a big threat to the Japanese Army?" I asked.

"The guerrillas were not a big threat, true sometimes they attack some of our troops. But to my knowledge, our soldiers did not kill any resident in those operations," he said.

"You were a general and a core member of the corps and yet you say you don't know of that massacre. He was taken aback. After a brief pause, I continued; The existence of that massacre is a fact. I confirmed it through my research here and in the Philippines. On top of that the corps headquarters did issue the order for subjugation and even forced the units to do so when they were hesitant to carry it out," I challenged him.

"I do not know about that massacre because my duty as a general of the corps was to "clean up" the headquarters as we were moving from Cuenca to Santa Clara, Batangas," he said coldly.

"Looking back at the past, don't you think each Japanese who was involve in the mass massacre by obeying the order is morally responsible?"

"Hmmn, I am not sure," he said.

He folded his arms and became silent.

"Do you feel sorry for the war victims in the Philippines?" I asked.

"No. That massacre was done by another unit and we have no link with that unit. In fact, I was sentenced as guilty in that unfair War Tribunal in the Philippines and confined in Muntinlupa for eight years. So I want them to apologize to me, instead of me apologizing to them," he replied.

"For which "guerrilla subjugation" were you charged?" I asked.

"The subjugation in Bai, Laguna, I was charged with torturing and killing more than seventy people. Itoh was executed even though he was innocent. The Tribunal charged him for bringing and killing those people in a coconut plantation farm. A Filipino witness came forward and pointed to Lt. Itoh and me. So, we were sentenced as guilty. It was ridiculous," he said.

"But there was a problem on the Japanese side, too. According to the posthumously published memoirs of Lt. Itoh, he wrote before he was executed that Lt. Suzuki of X Amphibious Battalion commanded the Bai subjugation. Though it was clear who committed that subjugation, why did the other Japanese allow Lt. Suzuki to return to Japan? There must have been a problem in the method of assuming responsibility in the Japanese Army?" I asked.

"Yes, there was a problem," he said.

"Do you wish to apologize to the war victims in the Philippines?" I asked him again.

"As I said before, I don't have such a wish. I was a victim, too. I was sentenced to death even though I was innocent. How can they compensate me for those eight years for which I severely suffered? If they continue asking me to apologize, I want to ask them to bring back my lost youth. We are equal since both of us suffered."

"But Filipino say, 'If the Japanese Army had not invaded us, such misery would not have happened.'

This misery was started by the invasion of the Japanese Army, wasn't it?" I asked.

"Invasion? I don't agree with your use of that word," he said in a disgruntled voice.

A Soldier's Diary: Sayama's True Face

A day after I met Seiji Sayama, I happen to get by chance a photo copy of Memory: Memoirs by A War Criminal by the late Genpei Tanaka. Tanaka participated in the "guerrilla subjugation" of Calamba as a platoon leader and was sentenced with thirty years of imprisonment as a war criminal. Later on, his term was reduced to fifteen years. While he was confined in Sugamo prison, his 187-page memoirs recalled his past. It was written in longhand. As read through his memoirs written in the style of a diary, I discovered the true face of Lt. Seiji Sayama who served under a general during the Second World War. The section titled: "February 12, 1945 Calamba Subjugation" describes his activity then: "Today we herded about 1,800 residents into a church as suspected guerrilla. About a thousand among them were released. We concluded then that the remaining residents, about 800, are guerrillas (members of Ganap identified them). We brought them by truck to a burning place and killed all of them. Today's subjugation was under the overall direction of Lt. Seiji Sayama, a member of the core of the corps" (Tanaka's memoirs).

After Japan's defeat in the Second World War, the investigation against war criminals began in November, 1945. So POWS decided to discuss how to answer and prepare themselves for their interrogation on the Calamba massacre with Lt. Sayama presiding.

"The plan of Lt. Sayama was as follows:

1. Direction

    1) minimize the number of soldiers to be convicted as war criminals

2) Measures

    1) deny the soldiers participation in the subjugation as much as possible.
    2) if it is inevitable to admit one's participation, use the following reasons:

        (a) It was ordered and directed by Capt. Saito, leader of the Los Baños Guard Unit, and other officers.
        (b) The executions were done by units under Lt. Yamada of the Lipa Flight Squadron and Warrant Officer Sato of MG Platoon (Note: Capt. Saito, Lt. Yamada, and Warrant Officer Sato were all killed in battles on Mt. Banahaw.)
        (c) To answer according to the above-mentioned reasons [(a) and (b)] and not reveal that the subjugation was ordered by the corps and directed by Lt. Sayama." (Tanaka's memoirs).

"We decided to conceal the truth by telling a lie. But this decision became a burden to me up to the end of my trial. I often had the feeling I'm standing up against a wall. It came as a matter of course that when I was forced to do so, I was nailed because of my statements."

"Lt. Sayama managed to evade prosecution because of my false testimony at that time (in the War Tribunal)."

"However, Lt. Sayama was charge as responsible for the Bai subjugation, although he had nothing to do with it. After we were sent to Sugamo prison, he was convicted in a Philippine court and given a death sentence. When I think of his situation where he is suffering in a prison in Muntinlupa, I could not help but reflect on happiness, misery, irony of man's fate and other matters. Even though you believe you are excellent, you're just a man. Your wisdom is just the wisdom of a human being. You cannot be god."

For there responsible for the Calamba massacre, four officers were prosecuted and Shozo Sato was sentenced to death in the first trial. And three other officers were sentenced with thirty years of imprisonment. But all of them were released through a special pardon in July 1953.

Because I wanted to interview with this three officers who experienced life in prison as war criminals other than Sato-san, I wrote to him to know if they are still alive. Though Genpei Tanaka, the author of *Memory* is now dead, the others are still alive in the snow country.

Sato-san wrote a postscript at the end of his letter to me. It said: "Those three were doing geographic research to build our encampment because the attack by U.S. Forces from Manila was forthcoming. They were prosecuted and convicted just because this happened to be in the suburb of Calamba on the day of subjugation. How could such a stipendous trial happen? I feel sorry for them." He did not tell me their names, so it was unclear for whom he 'felt sorry'. But because he used the word "sorry" and admitted that he was the commander when the Calamba massacre happened when I met with him previously, I presumed that he meant those other three officers were tried stupendously.

Soon, Sato-san called me up and said, "All of responsibility for Calamba subjugation was with me. And the other three officers had nothing to do with it at all." And he continued. "I called up Yukichi Yashiro who had been convicted with me as a war criminal for the same incident." Yashiro-san added, "While they complain now about what the Japanese Army did in the past, the guerrillas killed many Japanese, too. If we disclose these facts now, it will lead to a big international problem."

Because I want Yashiro-san to elaborate on his statement, "The guerrillas killed many Japanese," I wrote him a letter.

On 19 April 1945, the survivors from the X Infantry Regiment, the X Airfield Battalion, and other units started retreating to Mt. Banahaw, after fighting with U.S. Forces in a fortress in Mt. Malipuyo. Yashiro-san claimed many of Japanese soldiers had been killed in the battles fought between the guerrillas and the retreating Japanese Army during this period.

He sent the following reply to me.

"U.S. Forces perhaps thought that the retreating units had no ability to fight and did not pursue us. Their main force went away to help those units north of Manila."

During this time, the soldiers in units (of Japanese Army) lost their will to fight and were not able to fight courageously. And the units were divided into groups composed of small number of soldiers because guerrillas blocked the routes. I supposed they were easy targets for the guerrillas. The guerrillas formed into small groups and scattered around the vast area. Sometimes they blocked our routes or ambushed us. They also attacked the Japanese soldiers who were hiding because they could not move around in daytime as it was dangerous. And our exhausted and wounded soldiers were at the mercy of the guerrillas who know the terrain.

Although Yashiro-san wrote that: "The Japanese Army lost its will to fight and was not in a condition to fight courageously." But when they were ambushed the retreating but still armed Japanese Army engaged the pursuing guerrillas. That has nothing to do with the massacre of residents done in the name of "guerrilla subjugation" by the Japanese Army.

By the way, according to Sozho Sato, commander of X squadron, Yashiro-san had completely no role in the "guerrilla subjugation" of Calamba although he was prosecuted as a war criminal. But was it true? Gempei Tanaka wrote of the role Lt. Yukichi Yashiro, leader of a working squad of infantry XX Regiment.

On 8 February 1945, four days before the Calamba massacre, Tanaka placed under the command of Lt. Yashiro of the working squadron of the corps.

An entry in Tanaka's memoirs:

"February 12. Today's the day of the 'Calamba subjugation' which decided my destiny. Early in the morning, Lt. Yashiro ordered me, 'The squadron under Lt. Yamada must cooperate in the Calamba subjugation which the corps will conduct from now on. So, the squadron must secure the main roads leading to Calamba and patrol the town, to make it easy for the corps to conduct the subjugation there.' And I was given sketchy directions on how to occupy and patrol the areas. Then, I immediately mobilized my squadron and finished deploying them by sunrise."

"At 12 a.m., I received Lt. Yashiro's order to withdraw our patrolling unit and go to the church in the center of the town. The subjugation had ended," he said.

We arrived at the church at 1 p.m. . A thousand suspected guerrillas were confined at the church. Upon our arrival, I was ordered by Lt. Yashiro to give two squads to be placed under his command. I directed my remaining squadron members to watch over the suspects."

At 9:30 p.m., I arrived in our barracks. Soldiers staying there told me that the fire seen near us was the place of guerrilla execution. At 10 p.m. the two squads placed under the command of Lt. Yashiro returned to my squadron. They reported to me that they worked at the execution site," he wrote.

I concluded: "They worked at the execution site" means "they massacred those residents."

"At 10:30 p.m., Lt. Yashiro called me in the barracks. He told me about the subjugation conducted today, the policies of the corps on subjugation, and the method of implementation, which is as follows:

1. Considering the current activities of the guerrillas, the corps should implement total subjugation in the area they are patrolling.

2. Since it is impossible to differentiate innocent residents from guerrillas, we should assume that all the residents are guerrillas.

3. Therefore, except for those who are obviously cooperating with the Japanese Imperial Army, like the members of Ganap, we should kill all the residents, even women and children. And we should make the areas we are patrolling unhabitable so that we can fight our enemy easily.

4. Company commanders will recognize the contribution of a soldier who has killed more than ten guerrillas. Battalion commanders will

recognize a soldier who has killed more than thirty guerrillas. The Corps commander will recognize a soldier who has killed more than fifty guerrillas.

These are the policies of the X Corps commander. He ordered that the units which will conduct the subjugation should make a research on the area (to master its terrain)."

The Silence of Sozho Sato

A few days later, I went to Sozho Sato's house, armed with the note by Genpei Tanaka in my hand. He was the company commander of the unit which conducted the Calamba subjugation. He should know the entire story.

"Is it true that Lt. Seiji Sayama, a member of the core of the corps, was in command when the Calamba massacre happened?" I asked.

"Who told you about that?"

Sato-san said raising his voice as he focused his eyes on me.

I read the relevant parts from Tanaka-san's memoirs. After doing that, Sato-san tacitly affirmed the truth with amiable look, which to me reflects his good character.

"In addition, when Sayama-san gathered four officers, including you, held a discussion, all of you decided to put the blame on the dead officers, when it became clear that a military tribunal will try those involved in the Calamba massacre," I said.

"Ironically, Sayama-san could have evaded the responsibility on the Calamba massacre, but he was convicted for the Bai massacre which he had nothing to do with," I continued.

"His memoirs gave all that detail?" he asked.

"Yes. Though Sato-san said that Yukichi Yashiro had nothing to do with the "Calamba massacre", what he said was a complete lie, according to Tanaka-san's memoirs.

He smiled resignedly. I read relevant lines on page 31 and 32 of the memoirs, which describe the role of Yashiro-san in the massacre. Sato-san was nodding as he listened to me.

"Why do you have to protect Yashiro-san and the other officers?" Forty five years have past since the end of the war. Don't you think it is better to reveal that the indiscriminate massacre of residents really happened? As a group, why not think about how you can apologize to the victims who survived and the relatives of veterans,?" I asked.

But he said nothing. He just nodded a little to me.

"I concluded that the memoirs of Gempei Tanaka, was accurate in describing the participation of the Japanese Army during the "Calamba massacre", their court tactics 'always deny there was a massacre during the trials in the War Tribunal after the war, when Sato-san, tacitly affirmed the truth through his silence, commander of the X Company,

Sato-san told me in a subdued voice, as he sent me off at the station:

"I have added 'the war victims in the Philippines' in my list of war victims and I am praying for them every morning and evening."

FRANCISCO CASTILLO

Why don't the Japanese admit their crimes?

I make it a point to meet with Francisco Castillo whenever I visit Lipa, Batangas. I knocked on the old iron gate patiently, because his entrance gate was closed. He appeared in the gate wearing torn short pants. Perhaps he was weeding in his farm.

"Do you know that there are some Japanese who complain that they were tried unfairly in the War Tribunal in the Philippines?" I asked.

"I do not want to comment on the ruling given by the judges, but I get angry because the Japanese Army invaded our country and tried to kill all by claiming that they could not distinguish the guerrillas from the civilians. Not only the high-ranking officers who gave the orders but also the Japanese who followed it are guilty. As long as they were stationed in Lipa and have or have not participated in the massacre in Pamintahan and other barrios, they are still guilty; anyway, they killed Filipinos . . ., even though the exact place of the massacre was not accurately pinpointed when they were prosecuted. What are they complaining about? Why don't the Japanese admit their crimes? Those people are pitiful; they have lost their humanity. They have lost their capacity to reflect on themselves and apologize.

Francisco Castillo escaped from
the Pamintahan Massacre (in Lipa)

"I want to say to those Japanese. We the war victims in the Philippines, have much more to bear, much stronger that what you Japanese are complaining about. Many innocent people were killed. Our fields were destroyed. Our crops were stolen. Our houses were burned. So, we have a lot of complaints. Because of these, before you complain about the Filipino and the War Tribunal you should first look at those generals of the Japanese Army who gave the cruel and savage orders. Those who ordered the unjustified massacre of civilians actually made you war criminals. Because it was the Japanese Army that caused it, all must severely criticize your higher officers and responsible persons who ordered it. I don't think you can solve the problem by complaining about the Filipinos," he said.

Why are they still complaining?

When I visited Perguno's house in Lumban, I told him about the complaints of the Japanese on the War Tribunal in the Philippines.

"At that time, Filipinos were so angry they wanted to see any Japanese to be sentenced guilty. We hated the Japanese almost at an abnormal level. You know well what the Japanese Army did in Batangas, don't you? If you have come to this barangay to do research during that time, you might not have returned to Japan anymore. Filipinos' anger toward the Japanese has reached that abnormal level. As a result, there might have been emotionally biased decisions. Those judges were also Filipinos with emotions. But do you think it is right for them to complain on the War Tribunal despite the fact that they have killed so many residents in Lumban and Solok? The people in this barrio were massacred in the forest of Bulihan and Quemuros, but nobody was tried in the court of the Japanese Army. They were gathered suddenly and brought to a mountain stream to be killed. How do the Japanese think of this fact while they complain about the War Tribunal?" he said.

I asked him: "Do you know that a low-ranking soldier was convicted as a war criminal though he just witnessed the massacre perpetuated by his fellow soldiers in the Japanese Army on the other side of the river from the forest of Quemuros?"

"That's unfortunate for him, but he might have committed some crimes to the Filipinos in the other barrios. Although it might not be intentional, the Japanese deprived Filipinos of food. They had to do so to survive. I understand their situation. But because of their acts, it is a fact that many Filipinos suffered in food shortage. Even only for that, they deserve to be charged or sentenced guilty," he said.

"Do you know how many civilians were massacred in Lumban and Solok?"

"I don't know about Solok, but the number of those killed in barrio Lumban is 1,484. I know this number is correct because of a research conducted after Liberation. By the way, do you know how many Japanese were prosecuted and executed for the massacre of civilians in Lumban and Solok?" he asked.

I answered: – "Yes, I know. Four persons, including a second lieutenant, were convicted and sentenced to death by hanging. But through an amnesty, their sentences were reduced to life imprisonment. All of them were released in Japan in 1953," I answered.

He said: "Even though all of them have been freed, why are they still complaining? Filipinos are willing to forgive them, although their loved ones were killed helplessly. I want to stress to the Japanese youth that when its their turn to serve their country they must not commit such atrocites," he said.

A Lawyer's Verdict

I went to the house of Leonardo Alcantara in San Pablo after making an appointment. The Japanese Army planned to appoint his grandfather a mayor of the town during the Japanese Occupation. But because he declined it, he was brought to the barracks of the Japanese Army and detained there for one week. The previous puppet mayor had been killed by the guerrillas.

"My grandfather seemed to have been put in a dilemma, but he accepted the demand by the Japanese Army and became a mayor against his will. I do not know what happened in the barracks of the Japanese Army, I supposed he decided there was no way to survive except to do so." He spoke in English very fast.

I said: "The complaints by the Japanese found guilty as war criminals were completely unreasonable from the point of view of Filipinos. It makes no difference to them who was convicted or not. The massacres were committed by the Japanese, anyway — For example, there is the case of an officer was mistaken as the commander of those who did the massacre. He was prosecuted and eventually executed.

There are those Japanese, who symphatize with him and still complain that the military tribunals in the Philippines tried them unfairly."

"It was tragic case, but it is irrelevant to complain to the Filipinos and judges during that time, even though they mistook him as the commander. All Japanese officers and soldiers and Makapili, who collaborated to Japanese Army, were guilty. Even though an individual Japanese was a good person, such goodness of the individual is written off because the policy of the Japanese Army was evil from the point of view of Filipinos. During the war, an organization called the Japanese Army committed crimes against Filipinos. In the other words, Japanese and Makapili could not help but participate in war crimes within the organization called the Japanese Army that invaded other countries. View things this way and you will see that those who are complaining forget the fact that all of them are guilty," he said.

I said: "They also complain for another reason. Before deciding who is guilty, Japanese suspects were forced to stand in line. The one who is identified by the Filipino victims is prosecuted right away. But these Japanese are still angry because they were sentenced as guilty quite by mistake because of the Filipino inaccurate recall of events."

"Those Japanese have such complaints. The Japanese army gathered the entire residents of a barrio when a Japanese soldier was killed. They asked who is the guerrilla that killed that soldier. But nobody answered them. Then, they started to kill all the residents in that barrio without any further investigation. Such incidents happened quite often.

In San Pablo, 600 Filipinos with Chinese blood were massacred. When you compare their complaints with massacre of civilians, are those Japanese have the right to complain when they were convicted by mistake?" he said.

"There was another case of Japanese who has been a field commander in the resident massacre in Calamba. He could evade the responsibility for this incident, but he was prosecuted for the massacre of civilians in Bai. He served his sentence in Muntinlupa for a long time but after his transfer in Japan he was released. He still claiming that the military court in the Philippines was very unfair. What do you think of him?" I asked.

"He is crazy. He is from the point of view of Filipinos. It doesn't matter where he had committed his crime. He had participation in the Calamba massacre, didn't he? So many Filipinos were massacred in Calamba," he said.

"The memorial in Barangay Real says that 2,000 people were killed there," I told him.

"Yes, too many people, that's why it is unreasonable that the one who committed such massacre still complains. He lied, but God still see the truth," he said.

"By the way some Japanese assigned to fight in the Philippines said: 'We did some good but never committed any wrongdoing there.'

How do Filipinos regard such a statement?" I asked.

"That's their opinion. But as I said before, whether they intended it or not, by participating they became part of the institutional war crime by the Japanese Army. So they must be guilty, too. It is terrible because those Japanese did not examine their past fairly," he answered.

Then told me: "We worry about the recent military built up happening in Japan. If a war breaks up in Asia. She may commit the same mistake as what she did in the past. It is not only a problem for the Philippines but for other Asian countries, too."

They must reflect on their past conduct as if they were standing in front of God.

Antonio Nieva: Banzai?

Though it was cool in Lipa, Batangas, in Manila it was hot. I even felt a little pain on my skin when the sunlight peeps through between buildings. I thought this warm weather was typical in the Philippines anyway even with some nostalgia.

I visited Atty. Antonio Nieva who lives in Legaspi village, Makati City. He was an officer in the USAFFE and became a prisoner of war in Bataan. He was fortunate to have survived the "Death March". He went

239

back to Manila after he was released and started a business in tobacco trading. But because the Japanese Army tried to arrest him for the charge of spying, he escaped from Manila and joined the guerrillas.

"Did you know that some of the surviving Japanese Army are not aware that they were part of the invasion army, even though they were stationed here?" I asked.

"Is that true?" Perhaps because the Japanese had invaded China for a long time, they are still numb when they invaded another country," he said.

I said: – "I didn't know that we really occupied and oppressed other countries, I was one of those who thought that building a Great East Asia Co-Prosperity Sphere, means we have not really occupied and oppressed other countries."

"Did the Japanese believe in that propaganda? We were relatively faster in looking through the lies in that propaganda because what they did was completely different from what they said," he said.

I said: – "It was unbelievable but most of the Japanese believe the propaganda disseminated by Imperial Headquarters until the defeat of the Japanese Army. So, some Japanese still believe that the Japanese Army helped the liberation of the Philippines and other Asian countries."

"Some Japanese are very ignorant, aren't they? It was the Filipinos themselves who drove out Japanese army in various places in the Philippines to liberate our country, though the Americans helped us later," he said.

I told him about those Japanese who complain against the Military Tribunal in the Philippines. Then I asked his opinion.

"The decisions of the military courts were the expression of the emotion of the Filipinos. Almost all the Filipinos were angry against the arrogant, cruel, and animalistic behaviour of the Japanese Army towards the end of the war. The Japanese themselves who became animals know fully well what they did.

Members of the Japanese Defense Unit guarding Manila Bay massacred many innocent Filipinos. Some incidents also happened in Laguna and Batangas. Because they killed anyone as long as he is Filipino, they could be called—killers. It was a matter of course that the hatred by the Filipinos spread all over the country. Even though they made the biggest reason of the hatred, they are still complaining that the trials in Tribunal were unfair. Who on earth will accept such reasoning? I want to asked them: 'Did you make any investigation before you massacred a lot of innocent men, women, and children in Manila, Calamba, San Pablo, and Lipa?' Did you give them a fair trial in court? They killed indiscriminately, how can they say such utter nonsense?"

I want those Japanese to recall what they did in our barrios and towns in the past while they were fighting in the Philippines. And I hope that they will reflect on their past conduct sincerely, as if they are standing before God," he said angrily.

"Before you said that you don't want to work for the Japanese even when they request for you. Do you feel the same now?" I asked.

"Yes, I feel the same. I still don't like the Japanese." he said.

"Do you have any message to those Japanese soldiers who are still alive?" I asked.

"I never thought they would lived that long. Should I shout 'Banzai' to them?" he said and smiled mischievously.

Yamakawa's Wall

Toyozoh Yamakawa lived in a newly developed residential area in a city. When I finally find the entrance of his house, I found Japan's national flag, which he hoisted to celebrate a national holiday. When I said unconsciously, "that is unique". Also pointing to "The Emperor's View on Education" hanging on a wall in his room, "I am an admirer of the Emperor." Though there are some questionable lines in it, the respect to parents, the love between spouses, and other matters it can be used sufficiently as a guide for living even now," he said with confidence.

Yamakawa-san was one of the colour guards of corps headquarters. Colour guards are selected from several military units. He was stationed in Sta. Clara and Cuenca where the Corps had made it's headquarters in both.

"Did you happen to communicate with any Filipino during the war."

"No, not even once. I often guard the regimental flag, because it came from the Emperor. Besides, Filipinos are off limits to the headquarters . . . I have not talked with any of them," he said

"Do you often go to the Philippines for memorial services for your comrades?" I asked

"Yes, in fact I went there this year. I have gone there eight times already. I want to comfort the souls of my dead comrades. When I think of them, I pity them. If they were alive, they would have been married and have had children. They might even have grandchildren by now. But they were killed," he said.

I said: "I agree with you. But have you ever thought of memorial service for the Filipino war victims who were killed and whose country was made into a battlefield?" I asked.

"Yes, I thought about it. That's why we added 'For the souls of the dead officers and soldiers from the Philippines, Japan and America' by adding a few words." The Buddhist statue carry a dedication in English, 'For the peace and friendship all over the world.' We explain to the Filipino residents in the village that is a Japanese version of Mother Mary [Mother of God]," he said.

"I heard that the statue in Sta. Clara fell. Why did it happen?" I asked.

"I don't know who did it for what reason. I suppose it happened because the incoming and outgoing barangay captains has a conflict," he said.

– "Do you think it is possible that the residents did it because of their anti-Japanese feeling, because the statue was built near the massacre site," I asked.

"I think there wasn't a massacre committed there," he said.

– "Yes, there was in Bulihan, a few kilometers away from Sta. Clara, a massacre was committed on March 4, 1945. Many people were killed there while they were trying to evacuate," I said.

"Is that the truth? But it wasn't the XX Regiment, was it?" he asked.

– "It was the XX AirField Battalion. But from the point of view of Filipinos, the Japanese Army, whether it's the XX Infantry Regiment or the XXX AirField Battalion, both committed those atrocities," I said.

He said: "Maybe that's true, but . . ." He was hesitant to agree with me.

TOMOTARO UEMURA: A WAR MEMORIAL

With our apology oath renouncing war

I agreed to meet with Tomotaro Uemura again in a coffee shop in Shinjuku, in the heart of Tokyo. There is no strenght in his voice, I asked him why. He said his wife died only recently. He's already in his 70's and to lose a wife at his age I was afraid that he might be quite lonely. But from the way he looks, it seems he's okay.

After waiting for him to order a cup of brewed coffee, I started the interview: – "There is one thing I still cannot understand. Perhaps because I do not have actual combat experience in the battlefield. Why did those Japanese kill even children and babies? It is still incomprehensible to me, despite the order given to them to do so," I said.

"I was a civilian supporting the Army in the propaganda division. I also do not have any combat experience. But when I speculate their mindset, they must be determined to take revenge on the guerrillas, especially when their comrades were killed. It was like 'To hate the ground they tread on'. In fact, the matter on killing became cruel. It might be called as an abnormal war psychology," he said.

– "Was the corps pressured so much to conduct a "guerrilla subjugation" by all means? Do they sense imminent defeat?" I asked.

"I think so. In the case of San Pablo, the corps headquarters frequently pressured them to "subjugate" immediately. This time the American forces had already landed on Lingayen Bay. They were also attacked by guerrillas from the rear. Perhaps because the Japanese Army have not experienced any defeat, they have completely lost their normal frame of mind and became afraid and full of anxiety."

"That's the case with officers at the corps headquarters down to common soldiers?" I asked.

"If they were sane, they would not have committed such subjugation," he said.

I have another question: "Many of those Japanese soldiers do not want to talk about the massacre even after forty years has passed since the war, though they were involved in the massacre. They keep the secret in their hearts and want to bring it with them to their graves. Why do they behave that way?" I asked.

"One reason: they regret what they did. Another reason: they might be isolated from their comrades if they talk about it carelessly. And they don't want their family and society to know about it.

And if you talk about your experience of massacre in battlefield, you cannot sleep when you recall your past. It is very painful.

"Actually I also had a strange nightmare. In that nightmare, I was trembling in fear and went out to check if somebody has found a mass grave of victims. Maybe because I have seen dead bodies scattered around battlefield, though I did not participate in any subjugation," he said.

"Japan and the Philippines both became battlefields. But recently I think the nature of the battles in them differs, except for Okinawa. They fought on land in the Philippines. Don't you think that the damage from those battles will completely differ from those of air raids?" I asked.

"In what respect?"

"In all the subjugation by the Japanese Army, they always used bayonet for their massacres conducted in the southern Luzon area. When I asked the survivors and families of the Filipino victims, they do not remember anything about the moment when they were being stabbed as their mind were paralyzed by fear. Though the executioners and the victims were there face to face. As a result, the fear and hatred were deeply imbedded in the hearts of Filipinos by each Japanese soldier. At the same time, this is a fact that has deeply rooted in the heart of the Japanese Army, who committed the massacres, as an emotional burden, since he was splashed with blood of his victims. I think it became an unforgettable burden to every soldier.

"In this case the Japanese are victims, too," he said.

– "Yes, you're right. They too were victims, but at that time, they supported the army and the policy of the government, didn't they? In fact, at the time, I didn't realize it then I was one of them. I was also on the offending side," I disclosed.

"From the point of view of the Filipino war victims, what do you think do they think of the Japanese who are also suffering because of the war?" I asked.

"It is sad how they regard us. But they only view us only as executioners and offenders," he said.

"Even though how deeply Japanese are suffering, the Filipinos still consider us as animals," I said.

– "By the way, have you gone to the Philippines after the war?"

"Yes, I have. I have a friend in San Pablo."

– Some of the former soldiers went there for the memorial service for their comrades. Have you gone there with them?

"No, no way! . . . I have never gone there with them. It is a strange activity. I think it is wrong. They just pray for themselves with completely forgetting about many Filipinos, while their land was made a battlefield and they were killed. Americans were killed there, too. They do not think of them at all."

– "Why do they act like that in your opinion?" I asked.

"Their mind are limited by our narrow insularism. It is an isolated island mentality in which they can think only about their comrades and Japan. They do not have the international sense to think of the other countries' position," he said.

– "Do you think it is necessary for us, Japanese, to apologize to the war victims in the Philippines?" I asked.

"Yes, it is necessary. We should do so in a gesture of some kind. And we can build a memorial or monument with an oath renouncing war. Or we can write about our experiences during the war from the viewpoint of both Japanese and Filipinos to give our reflection on the war and to leave a record for the next generation," he said.

– "For example, if we give the money to build a memorial renouncing war we might forcing on them the Japanese way of thinking and design. However, if we squeeze Japanese way to them, the Filipino residents of the place may break down the memorial, instead of preserving and maintaining it voluntarily. What is necessary to erect a cenotaph so that the local residents love and maintain it carefully, and both of Filipinos and Japanese can swear war renouncing and pray for the soul of the war victims? How do you think?"

"It's important to consider the ideas of the Filipinos. It is necessary to consult them before you build a memorial where the Filipinos could offer prayers and flowers for their dearly departed. We should let them do its design and architecture."

– "Does it mean that we should just finance it but not get involve in its construction?" he asked

"Yes it should be like that. From now on, all of us Japanese should be broadminded," he said this with a beam in his eyes.

TAKAZOH KITABAYASHI: MY FILIPINO FRIEND

The treaty on war prisoner after we were defeated.

There was no stain on white shiny face, perhaps because he lives in snow country. Takazoh Kitabayashi is fat. He has been trained for seven years along the border between Manchuria and Soviet Union, to prepare the war against the Soviets, but he was suddenly transferred to the battlefront in the Philippines. He served in the corps headquarters there. He was one of those soldiers who retreated from Mt. Malipuyo to Mt. Banahaw and survived.

"Did you ever fight with guerrillas?"

"Experience in fighting guerrillas? Yes, I have. We guarded a field warehouse in Alaminos with less than ten soldiers. When I slept in the second floor under mosquito net, we were attacked by the guerrillas. But a barrio captain secretly told me about this guerrilla attack before it was carried out. It was because I became his friend by visiting his house everyday. He advised me to learn Tagalog language if I would stay in the Philippines and I learned it from him. Because he saved my life and I have been visiting the Philippines as much as fifteen times after the war. I bring him a gift everytime I visit," he said.

"I guess the memorial ceremony is mainly done by the Japanese. But do Filipinos also participate?" I asked.

"After offering food or flowers to the statue, Filipinos gather there first and burn incense sticks, too.

Then the Japanese made their offering, too. The local residents voluntarily participate in it, too."

But because the statue was struck down from the base in Sta. Clara, we asked the new barangay captain to rebuild it. Here is the design. He brought out a simple drawing. I found two sets of text: Memorial "For the Eternal Rest of Those Who Died Here" and "Memorial for Peace" in Chinese characters written parallel with the drawing of a rectangular stone. Perhaps they could not decide which sets of text to use.

"We want to build a a tough memorial so that it might not be destroyed again. And we will engrave a cross in it and we will invite a priest on a completion ceremony," he said

– "To whom will you build this memorial?" I asked.

"For Filipinos and Japanese," he said.

– "Do you think Filipinos understand Japanese language and its meaning? What do you think of using Tagalog language on it?" I asked.

"Then the Japanese cannot read it," he said.

"What about putting Tagalog text infront and Japanese at the back?" We cause them a lot of suffering by making their land into a battlefield. Or is it better to consult them on what kind of memorial to build? If you impose your design, they might destroy it again or it may suffer neglect.

"That's correct. I also think it is better to make something the local residents can pray and make offerings. It took several visits before the residents became friendly to us. We brought a lot of presents, too. This year we brought about sixty boxes of presents for distribution to various places," he said.

He opened photo albums for me. In one of the pages, I found a picture where it shows they gifted the pupils of Bai Elementary School with pencils. I suddenly remember one of the members of the group who went to the memorial service. He angrily said, "We gave them stationeries but they did not even thank us."

"Did Kitabayashi-san and you know about the massacre of civilians in Bai on February 9,1945 done in the name of "guerrilla subjugation?" I asked myself.

"Its possible to rule the people of another country with bullets, but economic power or power of money is effective. When we bring various things as presents, they welcome us happily and cooperated with us. As a result, we were able to build the statues," he said.

"What will you do when you are so old that you cannot visit the Philippines with presents anymore?"

"It would be a big problem," he said.

"What can you not forget in the Philippine battlefront?" I asked.

"The difference of our weapons greatly differ. Though Americans carried light rifles; we used heavy meiji 38-type (1905) rifles. They were made in Meiji 38 (1905) and impossible to use in the jungle. This is why the Japanese Army emphasized the spiritual aspect in our fight. That war was an unwinnable war, "After we were defeated in the war, I came to know that there is an international treaty for the treatment of war prisoner. Though the Japanese Army taught us to commit suicide instead of being caught as war prisoners, but we want to live. But they did not tell us of it and we did not know it, and many soldiers died, even though they must have lived longer. I believe we must renounced war forever. I returned to Japan in 1949. It was ten years after I applied to the army when I was eighteen years old. I didn't have any girlfriend, much more a wife. I didn't even have an experience to hold the hand of a woman. Because I had become too rigid and stiff while I was serving the army, it was difficult for me to change my character to milder one after I started my business. My previous character shows up even now after I had a drink," he bitterly smiled showing his white cheeks.

I remember his comrade saying, "He speaks like a military after he had a drink during our trips to the war memorial."

THE STATUE IN GREGORIO'S GARDEN

I got on a jeepney going to San Pablo from Bai. The jeepney was filled with passengers and climbed up a beautifully paved road. Coconut trees were planted up to the peak of the mountain range on both sides of the road.

The area was called Imuk hill and it had been a battleground between Japanese and Americans at the end of the war. More than 600 Japanese officers and soldiers were killed here in the battles.

The driver of the jeepney stopped in the front of the house of Gregorio Cusico. A new buddhist statue was built as if it was attached to the hedge of his small garden, which faces the main road.

Mr. Cusico works for a bus company. He was not home when I paid him a visit I talked to his wife instead.

"Tell me about the statue," I encouraged her.

"About that statue? It was built two years ago. Another statue was erected in the mountain before. They said it was because the Japanese soldiers had been killed and buried there. The Japanese began coming here to pray about fifteen years ago. My father gave them permission to erect a "Japanese Maria" because he owns the lands."

"What kind of ceremony the Japanese hold when they come here?" "They burn incense sticks and pray, in the Japanese style. They present us with gifts from Japan like cigarettes, wine and clothes. My husband attends the ceremony because he is obliged to do so, but few of our neighbors attend it," he said.

"Are you afraid whether the people in this barangay will complain about those Japanese who hold such ceremony for their dead comrades only? The war happened in the past, so no one is angry at them anymore."

A JAPANESE STATUE IN A FILIPINO GARDEN

Japanese hold ceremony as they please

Though I visited a new barangay captain, he was absent because he was working as a jeepney driver.

I visited an old man who had experienced the war. He was vaguely looking at cars passing by. Although he had been a member of USAFFE, he returned to his hometown without joining in guerrillas after U.S. Forces and the Philippine Army surrendered in Bataan."

"Do you know about the so called Japanese Maria?" I asked.

"What is that?" he asked back in low voice. "Are you talking about the statue built by the Japanese in Mr. Cusico's garden? Is that the Japanese Maria? Who gave that name? We have nothing to do with that. Though the Japanese come here from time to time to hold their ceremony as they please, nobody in this area attends it because we are not interested in it," he said.

"What's your opinion about the fact that they just hold their ceremony only for the souls of those Japanese, even though Filipinos were also victimized in the war?" I asked.

"Such behaviours, of course, unjust. But the Japanese seems to be unaware of it. So, I do not like the Japanese that much," he said.

"Kwannon", Japanese goddess of mercy, was erected by veteran Japanese army soldiers for the repose of the souls of fallen soldiers. Filipinos were made to believe it is a Japanese Mary, mother of Jesus Christ

Nothing I say will bring my father back

An old woman was looking at me from her house a few houses from that of Mr. Cusico when I passed by. As I felt something interesting with her, I looked back and called her.

"What is your unforgettable experience during the war?" I asked.

"Actually, my husband was taken away by the Japanese Army in the night. Until now he has not returned. Surely he was killed," she said.

She said without any emotion perhaps because the incident happened in the distant past. Her face was narrow and she just tied her hair streaked with gray at the back.

"I don't know why he was killed. He was brought away; while I was pregnant with my first child then. Since after that, I heard nothing of him. Though my husband was the only victim from this barangay, many were brought away and were also missing in other places," she said.

"Do you attend the memorial services by the Japanese?" I asked.

"No, I don't want to attend. Although the Japanese bring us gifts, I have not received any gift item," she said.

"What do you think about the Japanese who are only holding memorial service for their own comrades?" I asked.

"I cannot express my feelings well, although you can ask me about it," she said.

I asked her son who is sitting beside her: "What do you want to say to the Japanese."

"Nothing I say would bring my father back," he replied.

"How do you feel when you're looking at the memorial service conducted by my fellow Japanese?" I asked.

"I just look at them indifferently from afar, thinking the Japanese can do what pleases them."

My opinion, it is difficult for me to say it.

I got on a jeepney going to Cuenca from Batangas and arrived at Barangay Deta, after transfering to another jeepney. There is a statue done in the Buddhist-style (Goddess of Mercy) built by the Philippine Islands Group of the X Infantry Regiment on a hill in this barangay. The Japanese Army, mainly under the X Battalion of the X Infantry Regiment, and the 8th Army of U.S. Forces fought each other in this area.

I visited the house of a barangay captain. I was guided to a spacious room with dining area. The interior of the room was unified into white and it was as bright as dazzling. All the furniture in it was brand new. The house was built with the saving of his son who had worked for four years in Saudi Arabia.

"Do you asked me if anyone had been killed in this barangay by the Japanese Army? Yes there were. Twenty-one male residents were brought to barangay Ambon-ambon and killed there. Although two of them survived, they were dead, too. One of them was my elder brother. I am not sure when it happened, but I think it was in 1944 or in the early part of 1945. The Japanese Army selected young people in this area to organize a group to cooperate with the army. My elder brother was chosen as a leader. Because they didn't have weapon, they sharpened bamboo sticks to use in their training."

"The Japanese army asked them to dig a fox holes in a mountain and were brought there. But they were killed."

"The reason? I am not sure but perhaps they were shot dead because of the charge of guerrilla activity."

The Buddhist Statue in Barangay

In sitio Mambok, two kilometers away from here, about forty residents, including men, women and even children, were killed, except for two women. It happened after U.S. Forces landed in Nasugbu."

"What is your opinion about the memorial service held only by Japanese from the point of view of Filipino?" "Although I have my opinion, it is difficult for me to say it as a barangay captain."

"Is the visit of the Japanese Veterans' group beneficial or not to you?" I asked.

"Although they give some gifts to the residents who allowed the Japanese to build the statue, to the other residents, it's not much beneficial."

"Do you asked me what will happen to the statue after the Japanese become too old to come here with gifts? I cannot say what will happen. It is maintained now perhaps because the Japanese ask the residents to do so."

"Do you want to know about my experience during the war? I was confined in the barracks of the Japanese Army in Lipa.

It was when I stayed in a small house for vacation near a field. I was caught by the Japanese Army around 2 a.m. and brought us to Lipa. In the beginning I was detained by the Air Force Unit, and then I was detained in a barracks in the city. It was a place where we could hear well the sound of bells on the church. Then they started to torture me to know if I am a guerrilla. They punched me severely. They tied my hands behind my back and winded a rope around my neck to hang me down. Then, they took the chair away on which I stepped on and suspend me only with the rope. When I bent down my head, I suffered because my neck was choked. They also squeezed a burning cigarette on my body. When they struck a blow at me with a thick rope, I felt as if my left eyeball popped off. While I was confined for about a month, they gave me a food only once a day. Sometimes they didn't give me food at all. They did not give me water sufficiently, too," he said.

"Do you still hate the Japanese?" I asked.

"It is a difficult question for me. Because I am a barangay captain, it is hard to say what I am really thinking," he answered. I asked: "Do you think those Japanese who came here know the massacre of twenty-one residents and that you were tortured?" "Maybe not. Perhaps they don't know, because they seem to be indifferent in such matters," he said.

Flora Halina: memorial service for peace, memorial service for all

Upon the introduction of the barangay captain, I visited Ms. Flora Halina's house. She was the eldest sister in the family and the Japanese Army killed her father. Because she was still single, she lived with her younger sister and her husband.

"When my father was killed I was only thirteen. I am the eldest and there were four brothers and sisters. The youngest among us was only six months old," she said.

Her father was taken away from his house by the Japanese Army. And after he was brought to a mountain, he was killed together with other residents.

"Do you asked me how I feel about the Japanese who had killed my father? I heard that my father was killed not by Japanese but by Koreans. I heard that the senior officer in the Japanese army ordered to Koreans to kill my father."

"Do you want to know the evidence which shows that my father was killed by Koreans? I just heard so.

After my father was killed, my uncle and aunt supported us. Because we believed that my brothers and sisters would have received better education if my father had not been killed, we sent our youngest brother to college by helping him among ourselves."

"What's your opinion on the memorial services held by the Japanese?" I asked. "I don't have much interest in it. They just come and go in our town and we just look at them," she said. "What do you think is the proper way of holding the ceremony which Filipinos can also participate willingly?" "I cannot think of it right away. Those who suffered in the battlefield were the Filipinos. Do you think it is good to hold a memorial service for all war victims, including Japanese and Americans who were killed in battlefield?", she said.

"I agree with you. That's a good idea."

"She said. We should hold a memorial service for peace, not only for the Japanese." "I also agree with that idea," The husband of her younger sister said, after listening to our conversation."

Run to the Americans

I got on a jeepney from the Lipa market. When it passed through Lumban and crossed over a mountain stream, we entered Barangay Solok at the foot of Mt. Malaraya*. When I visited the house of Mr. Magaling, with whom I made friends, I saw black coffee beans dried in the garden as usual.

I went to Sta. Clara guided by Magaling. Our jeepney ran slowly on unpaved road with rolling side to side. The residents from Lumban and Solok were massacred in two places along this road and just near the mountain stream. Men, women, and even children, were among the victims.

When we paid a visit to the barangay captain of Santa Clara, he was not home. A bellied man naked to the waist and stayed in the neighbors started asking questions in severe tone, when he knew that I was a Japanese.

"For what purpose do you come here? Do you know what the Japanese Army did in this area during the war? They committed wrongdoings in various places. Really? Are you also making research on the massacres which happened in the evacuation sites in Bulihan and the forest of Quemuros? If so, I am not angry with you. But usually the Japanese don't know anything about the incidents."

The Japanese Army and the U.S. Forces did not fight a fierce battle in Santa Clara, during the end of the war, the Japanese Army placed a corps headquarters that had moved from Cuenca in the south. The Philippine Islands Group of the X Infantry Regiment built a statue to commemorate this fact.

Soon, one of the barangay officials came to us. He was accompanied with by a bellied man in his early fifties wearing short pants. When I asked about him, he said he is a policeman in this area.

We were led to the house of Gaudencio Bauligen, the former barangay captain. He was lying on the couch; he is recuperating after a high blood pressure attack, he has no difficulty in speaking and I was able to conduct my interview.

"Do they say that the statue was destroyed because there were some troubles in the election of the barangay captain? It is not true because we were brothers. So, I don't know why the statue was torn down. Somebody who still angry against the Japanese Army may commit it, although we don't know who among this barangay did it. That the statue was built on my land in 1983, but it fell down from its base six years later."

"Do you ask me if the Japanese committed massacre in this barangay during the war, while they massacred many people in Lumban and Solok, the neighboring villages? No, there was no massacre in this barangay, but I wonder if anybody hate Japanese even now. Before that statue was built, we held a meeting and told them, 'Even though you do not like the Japanese, you should restrain your emotion.' It may be possible that children hit it with something, while they were playing," he said.

"Was there anyone who opposed the plan during the meeting?" I asked. "No one. They agreed with my opinion; no one opposed it," he said.

"Do you say they could not express their opinion clearly because it was during the time of Marcos regime? But I don't think so."

"Do you want to know what would be the reason if the residents were angry against the Japanese?" "Here, the people suffered from forced labor. It happened only in this barangay, perhaps the possible reason they were angry was the massacre of civilians which happened in the neighboring barangays. There will be no other reason."

"Japan placed the corps headquarters in this barangay. Do you want to know my unforgettable experience during the war? Yes, I have. I was twelve years old during that time. My father was the barangay captain. One day he did not come home at lunchtime, I looked for him. A Japanese soldier slapped him twice. I was shocked and hid behind a coconut tree as holding onto it. I found the reason later. Because my father arrived late for the forced labor; he was punished.

"At war's end, the corps headquarters was transferred in this barrio. When the soldiers used our houses as their quarters, the villagers were forced to evacuate to other barrios.

"On the day they committed massacre in Lumban and Solok, the Japanese soldiers held rifles with fixed bayonets and the atmosphere was scary even in the morning. They entered each house and searched it. When the Japanese suddenly entered my brother-in-law's house, he jumped from a window. But those Japanese soldiers staying outside the house caught him. But luckily no massacre was committed here,"

"Why did they not commit massacre here although they did it in the neighboring barrios?" I asked.

"Perhaps because we often cooperated with them in forced labor. One day we brought baggage to the mountain. When the translator told us secretly, 'Let's run away right now,' we could run down the mountain right along and escaped. They did this after they reached the mountain. The Japanese dispatched spies to various places to know the activities of guerrillas and U.S. Forces with the assistance of a barangay captain. But although those who came back from the spy activities told the information to the barangay captain, the captain did not report it to Japanese Army and made the preparation to let the residents evacuate to the direction in which the U.S. Forces were coming. So, I think the Japanese lost a chance to massacre the residents in this area."

He showed me the Buddhist statue that had been torn down from its base and now placed in the side of a sink in the kitchen.

When I came out from the house of Mr. Bauligen after I expressed my gratitude, the bellied policeman in plain clothes also came out. It was the first time for me that a policeman hang around me during my research. I felt so eerie because I do not know the reason.

The Memorial

It took about forty five minutes to reach Caliraya cemetery by jeepney from my hotel in Los Baños.

Although I heard that the Japanese government built it, I saw the name of this place written on the concrete wall that stood at the left of the entrance and looked like a parament as 'Japanese Garden'. I found another English writing in the left corner of the wall and it was "The Japanese-style garden was made by the Memorial Garden Construction Committee." The name of Mr. Nobusuke Kishi was listed as a person in charge of the committee.

There was a heavy iron gate in the entrance of this Caliraya Garden. And a security guard was standing at the cabin in the left of the gate. When I asked him, he answered that an electric company hired him. I came to know the relation between this Japanese garden and the electric company later. Because the operators of this garden have been renting the place from the electric company, they also asked the management to the company.

After I paid an entrance fee, I walked under the big narra trees and turned to the left. And I crossed over a pond made in Japanese garden style. And then I climbed up stone steps to go out a resting place of this garden. There was a straight concrete road in a spacious place. A huge rectangular memorial, which was horizontally built faces the road. It was "The Memorial of the War Victims in the Philippine Islands". A granite stone box was place on the stones that formed three steps. And the following letters were engraved on the left corner of the memorial: Completed on March 23, 1973 by the Japanese government with the cooperation of the government of the Republic of the Philippines.

Liberato Villanueva, the barangay captain, was in his early fifties, but his cheeks sank down and the colour of his face was brown. When I shook hands with him, I noticed that his hand was coarse and hard like a stone.

"Do you want to know whether we have any complaints against the Japanese Garden" "No, we don't have any complaints in particular. Because it was built on the land of the NPC (National Power Corp.), it has nothing to do with our barangay. I heard that they have transferred the remains of Gen. Yamashita, who was executed in Los Baños."

"Do you ask me if my parents lived here during the war? Yes, they did. Although I did not experience the war because I was only four years old when we were liberated, I heard a lot about the Japanese Army. My uncle was also killed. Though he was a common civilian, he was killed with the charge of guerrilla activity. During the end of the war, Japanese became cruel and tried to kill any Filipino they found. My uncle and other residents could not endure their cruelty and secretly formed an organization to resist the Japanese Army. Although it was not a guerrilla organization, my uncle was still arrested and killed.

The Japanese soldiers were bad during that time. They stole rice, coconuts and potatoes forcibly from the residents. They even raped women. Now the story goes around that the wife of the barrio captain was raped during that time. Many were killed. Some were able to escape and survived but others were brought away by the Japanese Army and never came back.

"When I was a boy, my parents and other adults told us almost everyday what Japanese army had committed," he said.

"Did the barracks of the Japanese Army existed here?" "Yes, it did. And a small church was used for torturing suspected guerrillas. One survivor still live in this barangay," he said.

"Do you say that it is unfair that there is a splendid memorial garden only for the Japanese even though there were many Filipinos victimized? Well, Filipinos could not comment on that because it was built during the Marcos era,"

"Do you want to know if the residents in the barangay agreed on the construction before the memorial garden was built? Perhaps they didn't consult even with the barangay captain during that time. It was the time of Marcos. We don't know anything because NPC, the owners of the land, made an arrangement with Japanese government by themselves. They never consulted the ordinary people during the Marcos era."

"Do you want to know whether it is better to inscribe the words in Tagalog language, if they will build a memorial in which Filipinos will be able to pray sincerely?" "Yes, of course. And the relations between the Japanese and the Filipinos will improve."

"I hope that no matter how good the project is they will not decide only with high-ranking officers like during the Marcos era."

HILARIO DETAN: TORTURED

I have not gone to such place

He was introduced by the barangay captain. I decided to listen to the experience of Hilario Detan, an old man. He had been tortured by the Japanese Army.

Because he was almost ninety years old, he came to the living room in the house of the barangay captain on feeble foot step wearing a blue hat.

"I had various experiences during the war. My house was burned down. And when I could not find my carabao, I believed it was already eaten by Japanese soldiers."

He continued speaking in mumble.

"It was a terrible torture. Japanese army captured me and brought me to their barracks. In the beginning I was hanged and punched repeatedly. Then they placed the handkerchief on my nose and mouth. Then they poured water on it. Because my hands were tied, I was nearly suffocated."

"The reason of this torture was that they suspected me of doing guerrilla activity. Even though I said I was not a guerrilla again and again, they did not release me."

"Later on, I was confined in a small chapel, because they used it as a prison house. While I was confined in it more than a week, I became very weak.

And because my eyesight was weakened, too, I could not see well even when I came out to a lighted place. I had an illusion as if the stars were falling down from the sky."

Because I was already married, my wife brought me food. But they prohibited me from eating anything; thus I suffered from hunger. They did not give me even sufficient water. So, I was almost weakened to death.

The entrance to Caliraya Cemetery

"When I was freed at last and went out on staggering footfall, a fat officer of Japanese army found me. Because he asked me, 'Are you a guerrilla?' I answered, "No, I am not." Upon listening to my answer, he pushed my belly once with the tip of his Samurai (Japanese sword) covered in its sheath. Because I was weakened, I fell down there."

"I remember now then that a Filipino was confined together with me and that he never came back after he was brought away by the Japanese soldiers."

"Do you want to know whether I am still angry at the Japanese? No, I am not angry at them anymore. Because Japan has joined hands with America and because the Philippines is a democratic country and has made friends with Japan, I am not angry anymore."

"Should those Japanese come here to apologize to you, will you forgive them?" I asked.

"I will forgive even the Japanese who hit me with his undrawn samurai when I was so weak," he said.

"About the Japanese Garden? I have not gone there!"

"Why"

"The reason? That has no relation with us," he said as he pouted his lips as if he was angry and looked away from us.

A Japanese Garden

When I returned to Japan, I read the speech by then President Ferdinand Marcos when he attended the opening ceremony of the Japanese Garden.

"Thirty-four years ago, the people in Japan and the Philippines fought each other. Japanese soldiers came to our land and they tried to fulfill their mission to conquer us by arms in the name of "sacred war" for the Emperor."

"This memorial remind us the price of the mistakes in the past and the price of the war victims."

"They just came here not for the friendship with us but to the desire to conquer us under their rule. Why should we pay respect to them?"

"This is my motto. 'We must be always generous, in defeat in challenge and in victory.' Today, the people of the Philippines and Japan continue forming a friendship in this spirit."

"Today when the relation between this countries has turned for the better, we may save the soldiers of the enemy who shed blood and fell down in our land from the bottom of tragedy, as we experienced and survived that war. We may revived that figures in our memories with generous heart."

"We can achieve the heart of generousity through the experienced sufferings."

Former President Marcos made an appeal to pray for the souls of the dead officers and soldiers of the Japanese Army that invaded the Philippines with generous and forgiving hearts.

I thought that this formula was not intended for the Japanese who attended the ceremony, but it was to pursue the war victims and people in the Philippines to settle down their anger.

The Japanese government built a Japanese cemetery to entomb only Japanese casualties of the war in the Philippines that Japan used as battlefield. And the Japanese supported this project from behind. How do they think of their past while they trampled other Asian countries with military boots?

The memorial for the war victims in the Philippines

POSTSCRIPT:
THE AFTEREFFECT

Miss Maricris Sioson, a Filipino dancer, died in Japan in 1991. The people in the Philippines looked on Japan suspiciously about the caused of her death. Her mother appeared in a television news program called News 21 by NHK on October 21, 1991 and said with anger and sorrow, "Japanese killed many Filipinos during the war. And now they killed even my daughter."

While I am researching Filipino experience of the war in Laguna and Batangas provinces in the southern part of Luzon Island, I was astonished with the fact that many of them still deeply distrust Japanese.

It is because Japan has not taken responsibility on the war in the way satisfactory for the war victims in the Philippines. Although Japan paid war reparations to the Philippine government, the victims of the war has not received even one peso of compensation. And Japan has not apologize sufficiently also in moral aspect. In early May of 1991, Prime Minister Kaifu put almost full page advertisement titled "The Profile of Prime Minister Toshiki Kaifu" on Manila Bulletin, a Filipino Newspaper in English, when he visited Manila to see off a minesweeper vessel of Japan's Self Defense Force. The most of this advertisement was covered with personal history and achievements. The words of apology were just added as if it was just a token under the picture in which he lifted his right hand.

Although it is already too late, the government of Japan has to apologize with sincerity to the people in the countries that Japan invaded or colonized. I believe that the apology will be meaningless if it is express without compensation.

While I continued interviewing with Japanese who had acted as executioners, I noticed that most of them hid the fact of the massacre of civilians deeply within their heart and that they did not reveal it even to their own wife. Because they were forced to act as bloodthirsty killers who stabbed the residents with bayonets and were drenched with blood on their whole bodies, they also have deeply wounded feelings no matter how tough they talk to their comrades and this writer. When we consider this aspect, those Japanese were also the victims of Imperial Japan in one sense.

Although they were victims, they recognize themselves as executioners. Many of those Japanese whom I met are living in the idea forcibly imposed in the period before and during the war. They have stopped examining the values themselves.

The most critical among such thoughts is the belief that "the guerrillas started the war on us". They still believe that the cause of the implementation of massacres of civilians done in the name of "guerrilla subjugation" was the anti-Japanese movement in the Philippines. The Japanese Army created the reason why the Filipinos are attacking us, the Japanese soldiers didn't understand the reason. In other words, some of the Japanese who lived in the period during the war are completely unaware about the simple and clear fact that Japan invaded the Philippines. Our government, which prepared and carried out the wars for invasions, required such kind of person and molded them intentionally through our educational and military systems.

And I felt uneasy while I was talking with those Japanese who had acted as assailants. It was because they justified their resident massacres by defending themselves through the claim that "I was ordered to do so and I had no choice". Although it was during the war that they killed people including women and children. I worked as a radio survey soldier for navy in a base in Japan during the war. If I had stationed in the Southern Luzon, I had participated in resident massacre to obey the order to "make the battlefield uninhabitable". But I believe we could have viewed our past objectively, if we detach ourselves from our war experience in the past fifty years since the end of war.

Filipinos claim, "Even though they were ordered, it is a matter of conscience whether they kill even women and children." We have to be intelligent enough to look back our past, discern if the order by our senior officers (the Emperor, being the highest) must be followed at any cost, from the present time.

And I wonder whether we accept what was repeatedly said "they had no choice" and keep silent. If any country had used Japan as a battlefield for ground battles resulting in its devastation and massacred the Japanese, as the case in the Philippines, what would we feel? We must remember the voice of the victims and sincerely understand in our hearts that their problem is also our problem.

I pointed out the selfish attitude of the Japanese who witnessed, participated and lived during the war period. Some Japanese said, "If it is inevitable to start a war, it must be started outside Japan" and "I never want to see my hometown become a battlfield." Because these Japanese (former officers and soldiers) knew and directly expressed war, they remember vividly in their hearts and minds the devastation and misery they caused. At present, Japanese visit the Philippines to hold a Japanese style memorial service only for their comrades. It is truly ironic because it was these Japanese who made the Philippines a battlefield. It was the Filipinos who suffered most, many were tortured and killed for unjustifiable reasons. Americans soldiers were also killed in that battlefield. Can we not hold a memorial service and build a memorial to commemorate all the victims of war and pray for their souls regardless of their nationalities?"

The self-centered attitude is not only seen in our war generation but also in our government. And this reality was manifested in this book. This thought shared by both our government and people support the policy of Japanese government to keep its responsibility on that war ambiguous and unwillingness to apologize and compensate to the victims of the war in some way.

The negative legacy left by our generation becomes a burden to our younger generations that live in the age of globalization. And it has not been overcome yet. As matter of fact, it still survives incorrigibly in other form. It is said that ODA or Official Development Assistance from our government to the countries in the Third World started from the payment of compensation in 1956 in the case of the Philippines. But this assistance is questioned because it only benefits Japanese companies and leaves only debts to Filipinos in reality. Some of Filipino critics even claim that the policy of the Japanese government and companies is "the second invasion".

A small number of war victims and their relatives are still angry and say that they will not forgive the war crimes committed by Japan until they die. However, the majority of Filipino says to the Japanese, "We are not angry anymore because it happened long time ago during the war" and "I forgive them as a Christian following the teaching of God." But I believed that we must not consider by ourselves that they pardon the war crimes committed by the Japanese Army in the past with relying on their words. We must not forget the conflict in the heart of Miss Fely Olerio, a resident of Los Baños, as a Christian, after she was wounded with bayonet and his younger brother was killed in front of her.

Those who can not forgive the war crimes by the Japanese and those who have already forgiven them shared the same belief that "We will not forget our experience during the war as long as we live." On the other hand, the Japanese do not even know what happened in the Philippines while the Japanese Army occupied it. Although the Japanese had to act as executioners, they wish to forget their conducts completely without telling the truth to any one. How can we bridge the gap between the victims and the executioners?

The image of the Japanese for Filipinos living in self-supporting rural areas has not changed at all from that of the Japanese soldiers during the occupation by the Japanese Army. They remember with strong impression and teach their children that Japanese were violent foreigners who had weapon and walked arrogantly and that they were cruel people who threw a baby into the air and stabbed him with bayonet as he fell down. Although I do not know if this incident was true, I often heard it even in Manila as a symbol of the cruelty of the Japanese Army (Japanese) .

It will take more than a century to wipe out the basis of such sentiment from common people. The duty to deal with the aftereffects of the war will continue to the time of our grandchildren and great grandchildren.

I have something to write for the honor of Koreans. A baseless rumors has spread in various areas of the Philippines as if it were true. This rumor is: "Koreans soldiers were more cruel than the Japanese soldiers." Whenever I hear of this rumor, I checked who said it. But the residents replied to me with vague answers like, "I heard it from a Japanese soldier" or "Everybody claims it." But when I think on to whom this rumor is advantageous, I think that I can see through the root of this rumor. As long as I made researches on the war victims in Southern Luzon area and the Japanese who had to act as assailants, I found no evidence to support this rumor at all.

Finally, I am thankful to the Japanese and Filipinos who cooperated with me in my research. I hope that your painful past will become a foundation stone to develop the peace and friendship in the future.

Demetrio Antonio, Marciano Magaling, and the Author

APPENDIX

* AUTHOR'S NOTES . . .

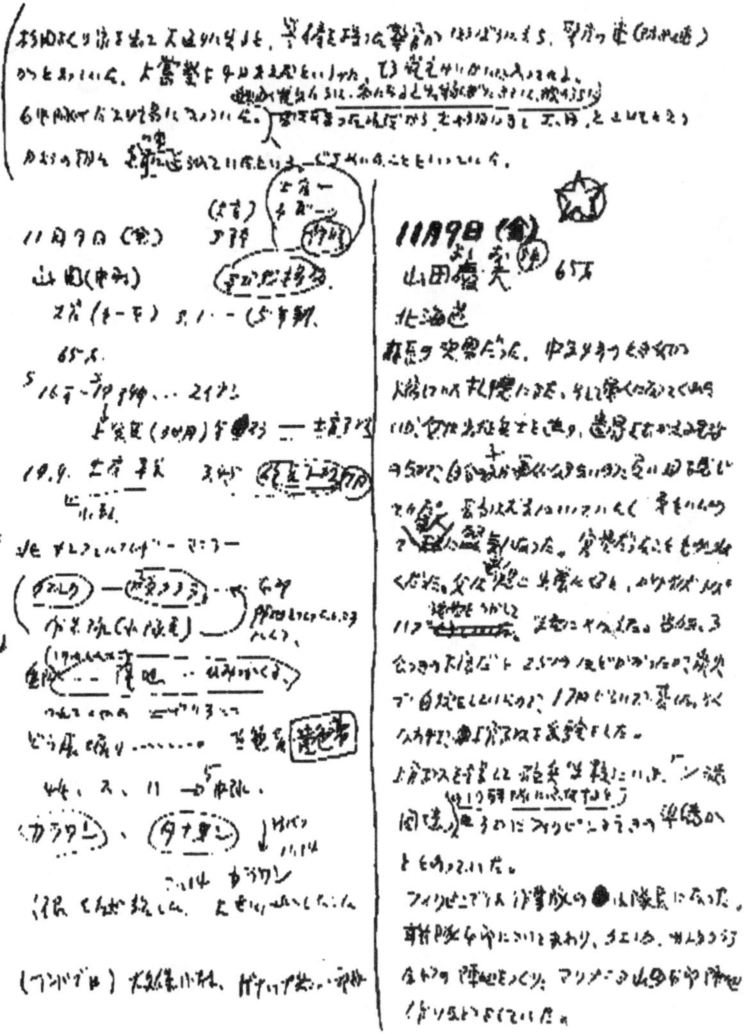

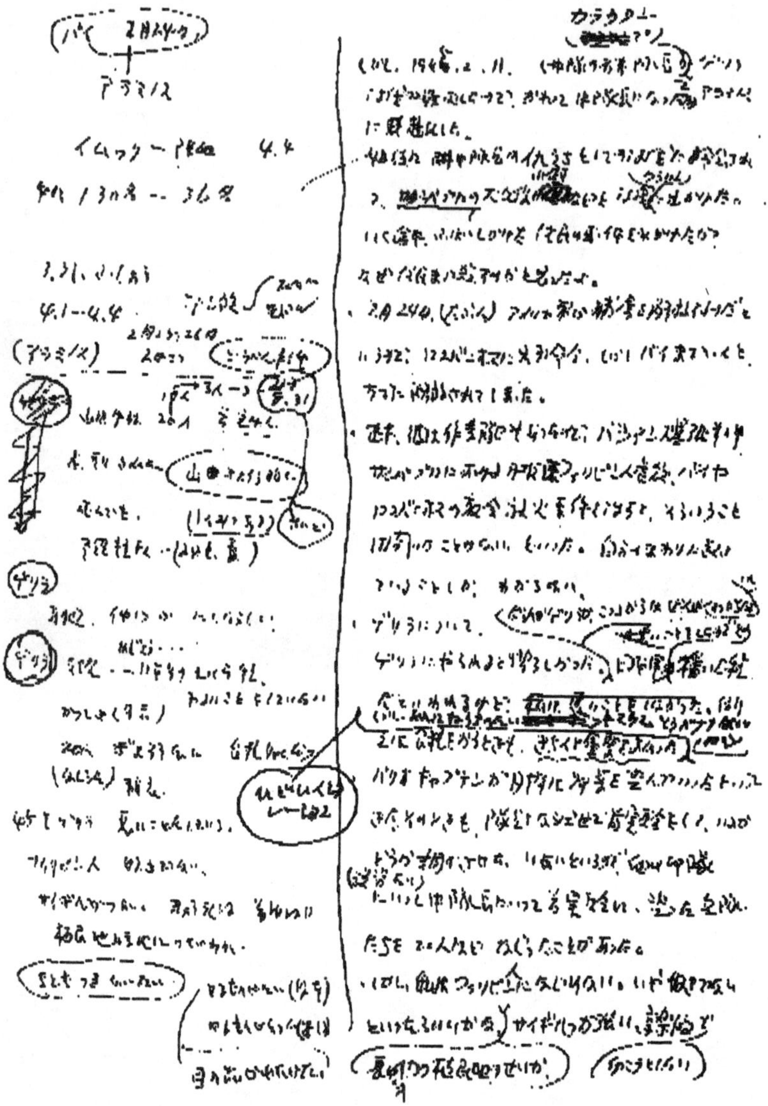

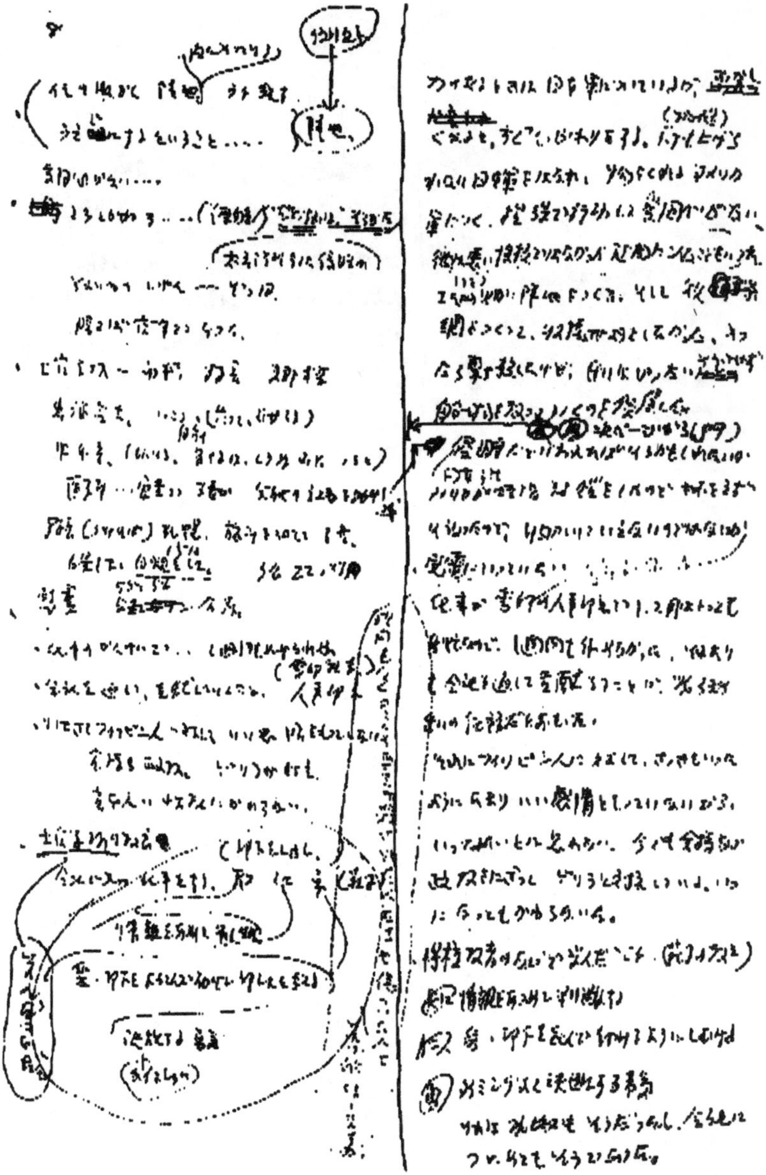

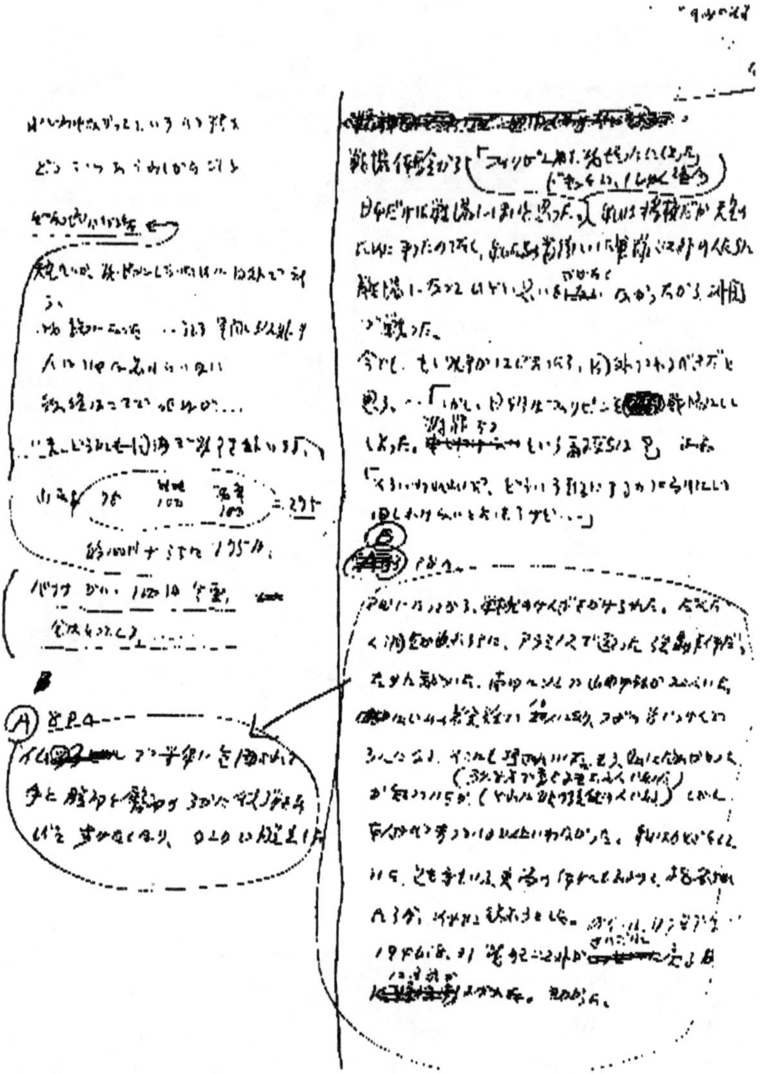

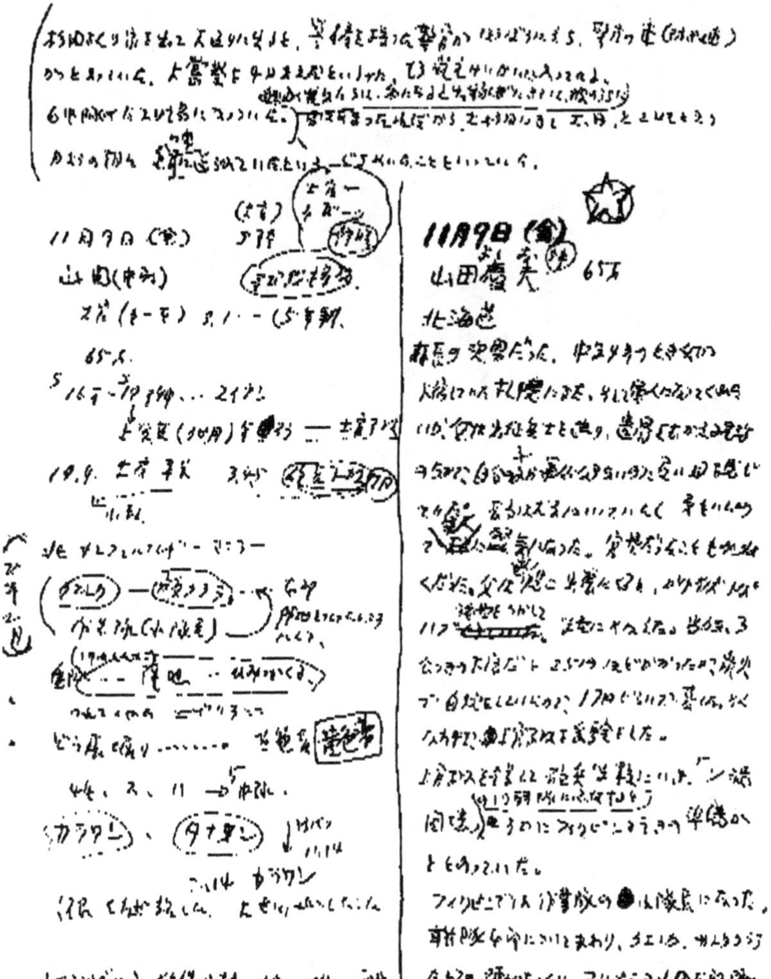
11月9日（金）
山田
65才
北海道

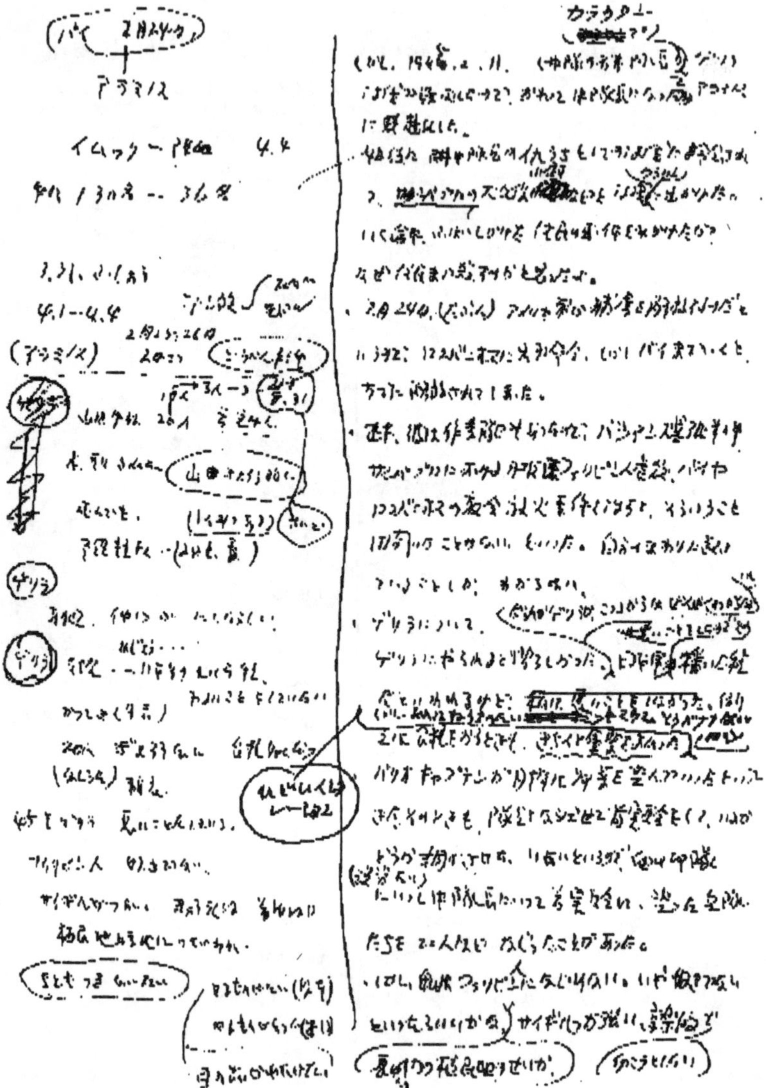

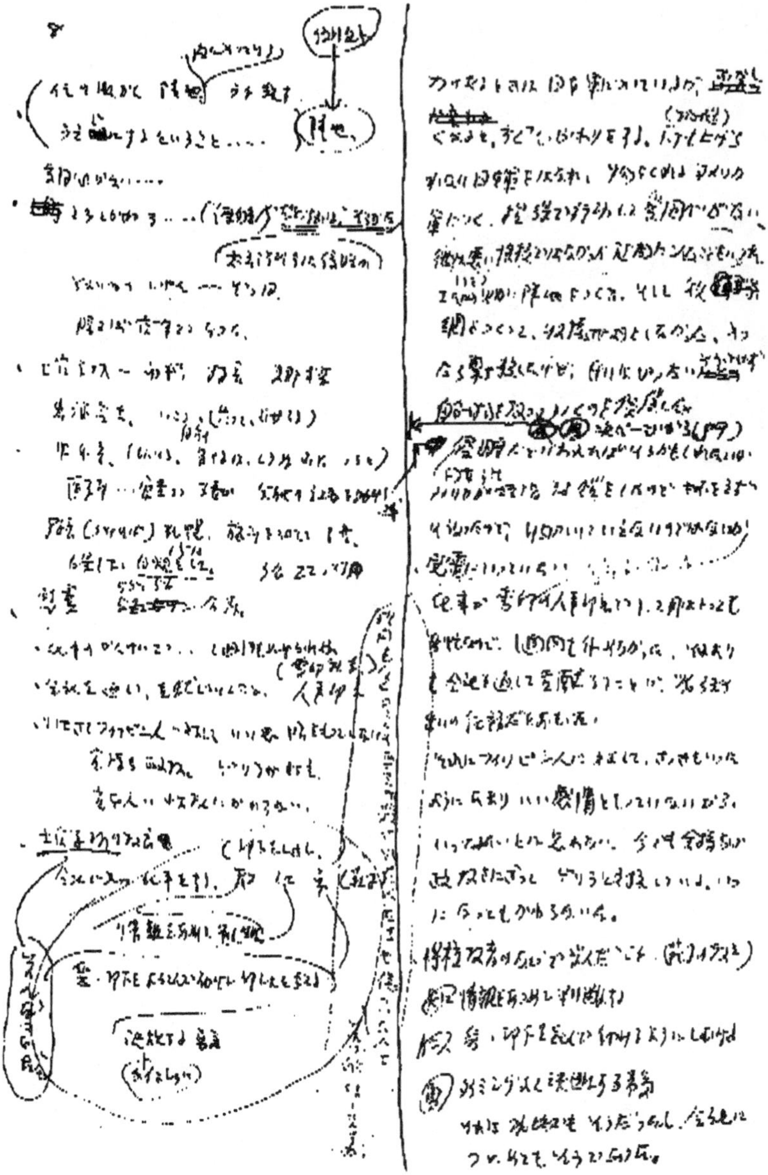

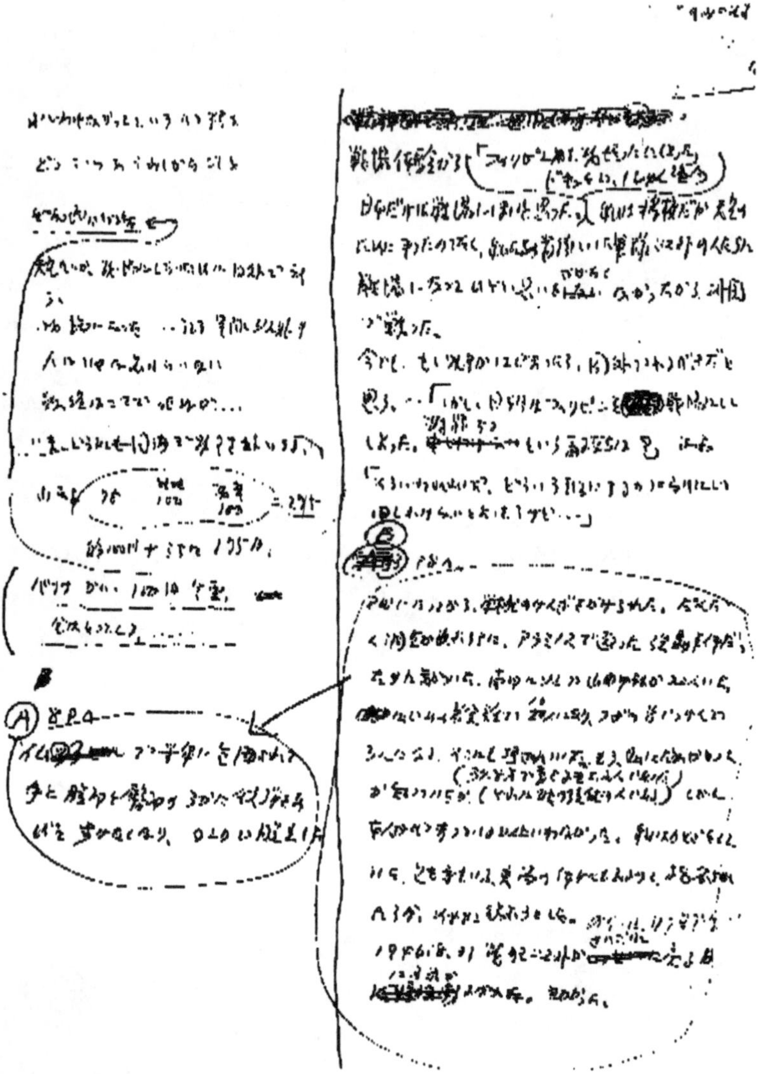

* **Texts lifted from Author's notebook**

• TRANSCRIPT

NOVEMBER 19 (FRIDAY)

MR. MASAHARU UEDA, 65 YEARS OLD
Hokkaido

Masaharu Ueda is the second son of a village mayor. When he was in fourth year high school, he went to Sapporo where his father stayed before. His father wanted him to be a soldier. As a mayor, his father attended ceremonies either to send off to battlefields young men in uniform or to welcome home returning soldiers in body bags. Understandably, his father was possessed with a sense of guilt seeing that his sons were comfortably in school instead.

Masaharu had two siblings — an elder brother who was already in college at that time, and another one who was much younger than he. Naturally, among three of them, he was the only qualified to be enlisted into the military. Nonetheless, he was happy to know that his training in the Military Academy was at government expense.

Whenever his father went to Sapporo on official business, he would eat nothing but the simplest meal of rice noodle soup to scrimp for extra money for Masaharu's subsistence allowance. At that time, board and lodging cost about 25 yen, but Masaharu had chosen to stay in a room without meal services for only 17 yen. He preferred to cook for himself using charcoal.

Masaharu's earnest, lifestyle managed him to survive the Academy. Upon graduation, he proceeded to an Artillery School and thereafter was deployed to the Russian border. Later, he was moved to the Philippines.

He become a commander of an engineering company in the Philippines, receiving instructions from the Regimental Headquarters. Among others, he built the military camp bases in Cuenca, Sta. Clara, Mt. Malipunyo, and others.

However, on February 11, 1945, Commander Ishii of Company No. 5 was killed in action. Masaharu Ueda assumed the vacated post and consequently transferred camp to the town of Alaminos.

After 4 days, he was ordered to go with Lt. Okubo and others to San Pablo to avenge the death of Commander Okubo in the hands of guerrillas. Along their way, he saw many decomposed bodies of residents. Silently he wondered why ordinary people had to die.

Perhaps it was in February 24 when he learned that the US Army was coming to rescue prisoners-of-war. He received an order to move to Los Baños to stop them. But on his way to the town of Bay, he heard of news saying that the mission had been accomplished.

Since he was member only of an engineering company, he denied any knowledge of bomb explosions in Bauan, massacre of Chinese residents in

San Pablo, massacre of churchgoers and burning of churches in Los Baños and Bay. Nor could he say anything about other military platoons and companies. He maintained that he could only recount what actually happened to himself.

He expressed his hatred for guerrillas particularly over the killing of his comrade but he admitted that he could not distinguish a guerrilla from ordinary people. He recounted: *"Many people said that the guerrilla movement became active because of the attitude of Japanese soldiers. But I did not do anything bad. For example, when I needed food, I always paid with war notes. When the barrio captain complained that Japanese soldiers stole their camote, I ordered all my men to line up for him to identify the culprits. When he could not point to any among them, I asked another company to line up too. When he finally recognized 20 soldiers from the line up as the perpetrators, I beat all of them."*

"However, I could not grown fond of Filipinos. Yes, I did not like them at all. Because of the long period of their existence under colonialism, they have become suspicious, epicurean and lazybones."

"When the Japanese Army was in power, they were following us, but when we were defeated, they changed their mind. Due to resource constraints, the Japanese Army could not give them anything so they shifted their loyalty to the Americans who had more logistics. They did not have patriotism. They were motivated by personal gains."

He tried to prove that he had been a good military officer through this story. *"We placed wire fence around the camp because we did not allow entry to Filipinos. If they trespass to harvest vegetables, the order was to shoot them. Nevertheless, I did give permission for them to enter so they could harvest."*

"You said that it was a case of Japanese armed aggression. But it was the Americans who started it. U.S. imposed an economic blockage against Japan to force us to open up. You cannot put the blame solely on the Japanese Army."

Since the end of the war, Masaharu never joined the memorial service trip to the Philippines. As the incumbent director of the personnel section of a private company, he cannot excuse himself from work even for a week. The trip to the Philippines is traditionally out that this post-war duty is to contribute in society through the private company where he is presently employed.

"And I told a while ago, I did not have any affinity with Filipinos. So I do not long to visit the Philippines. Until now, that country is dominated by a few rich persons, and the guerrilla movement is still alive. There has been no change in that country."

"In the Military Academy, I learned the Teaching of Confucius which are knowledge, benevolence and courage. I make good use of these teachings as a military officer and director of a private company. Knowledge means judgment based on appropriate information. Benevolence is to prepare a conducive

work environment for my own staff. Courage means decision with good timing."

Based on his experience in the battlefield, he said *"I don't want Japan to become a battlefield. I was a military officer, but I do not want to fight for the emperor. I fought for our country, people behind Japanese military. I fought in a foreign land because I want to prevent the war from coming to Japan. If war is necessary, we should fight outside our territory."*

Mr. Ishida: I have a question for you. In your own thinking, why did Japan make the Philippines a battleground? Do you have any intention for atonement?

"In a sense, well, I also feel sorry about it. But I don't know in what form . . ."

When he became a prisoner of war, he was charged with the commission of war crimes. During the hearing on the case, he learned that it was about an alleged rape incident in Alaminos.

At the outset of the investigation, the list of suspects included some 20 Japanese soldiers with the surname "Ueda" who where all stationed in souther Luzon one time or another in the duration of the Japanese occupation. After the victims came face-to-face with the suspects in a line up, the list was trimmed down to 10, and eventually to only 3. He remained constantly one of them. He knew who the real criminal was *(i.e., 37 or 38 years old, had a wife and children)*, but that person kept his silence during the trial. So

Masaharu Ueda kept quiet too. He prepared himself to be called to the witness stand. Because he had 2 – an elder and a younger – brothers who could still help his parents, he simply readied himself to accept whatever the court's decision was going to be. On August 31, 1946, he was found innocent and his name excluded from the list of war criminals. He was saved, he told himself.

* Unedited English translation of Author's notes

• QUESTION AND ANSWER

CALAMBA

1.   **Mr. Luciano Alcantara** (60 years old), male wears a pair of black eyeglasses.

Suspecting that a group of guerrilla was hiding in our home in Calauan, a Japanese soldier who was in pursuit of the guerrilla barged into our house and started killing everybody on sight. Five members of my family were killed including my wife and two children. I was spared only because I was out of the house then. I could have continued hiding, but the death of my family drowned me to a deep depression that I could not make myself do anything rationale.

Q.   When I had the chance to interview the former Japanese soldier, he explained that he could not distinguish among the people in the house who were guerrilla or who were not. And so he decided just to kill them all. How do you feel about this?

A.   It was wrong, really wrong. They were innocent people who happened to live in the said place. They were not guerrillas.

Q.   A soldier who witnessed the incident said that the order came from a senior officer and so he had no choice but to follow the order. What can you say about this?

A. I don't think that was the situation. But just the same, they have no right to kill innocent people.

2. **Mr. Dionisio Dalisay** (67 years old). Although he is already 67 years old, he looks much younger with his black hair and confident stance. He was 18 years old at the time of the massacre were his wife, mother and 10-year old son were killed.

Q. Please tell me what really happened.

A. The people of Barangay Sta. Flores in San Pablo, Laguna grew scared of the Japanese when two of our neighbors were killed by a group of Japanese soldiers who were in patrol. They were about to evacuate en masse from the village when the Japanese soldiers were alerted and decided to kill all the residents of the village of about 150 people. I was fortunate to escape the massacre since I was bedridden due to a debilitating sickness. However, I was captured together with seven others who were not able to run away due to either old age or some disabilities. Later on when the security was not that tight (with only two guards on duty), my father and I were able to escape from the Japanese.

Q. Do you have any message to the Japanese people?

A. Please tell them, especially the younger generation to learn from the mistakes of their fathers and grandfathers by not repeating the atrocities committed by the Japanese to my people such as the massacre of innocent civilians.

Q. Some of the Japanese prisoners of war claimed that their trial in Manila was not fair and impartial. In fact even innocent Japanese soldiers who were not even assigned to the places where the massacre occurred were adjudged guilty. What can you say about this?

A. I believe justice was served. While they claim not to have participated in the said massacres, they were as guilty as those identified to have committed the crime. The crime is not an individual crime committed by an individual Japanese soldier, but a crime committed by the Japanese Imperial Army as a whole to the people of my country. And so all of the Japanese soldiers should be considered guilty of the crime.

3. **Mrs. Alegoria Pyron** (77 years old). (She and one of her two daughters came to see for this interview)

Her husband was the victim. She only learned about the death of her husband after two months of his absence. In fact she doesn't even know where and why her husband was killed. But a friend said that the murder occurred somewhere in Batangas.

Q. Do you still hate the Japanese?

A.1. No, I guess it's because of my religion. I am a Catholic.

A.2. (Daughter) I can't remember anything about my father. I only saw him on a picture.

Q. How about you, have you forgiven the Japanese soldier who killed your father?

A.2. Yes, I have already forgiven him. That was a long time ago.

A.2. My daughter works for the International Rice Research Institute (IRRI), an international organization supported by the Japanese Government.

Q. Please feel free to express what you really feel inside?

A. . . . . . (No answer)

4. **Mrs. Lita Pontanosa** (62 years old). She is small and very slim. She was with her daughter who I later learned to have a Japanese friend.

Her husband was the victim. She remembered that they were talking their lunch when a member of the Makapili came to their house and asked her husband to come with them for an alleged meeting at a school nearby. As narrated by her husband to her later on, as soon as they arrived in the said place, they tied his hands behind his back and he was placed inside the garrison. There were others like him in the garrison with their hands also tied behind their backs. After learning of his husband's incarceration she frequently visited him and brought him food, but the soldiers refused to give the food to her husband and instead feasted on the food themselves. Later on, she learned of her husbands death but she doesn't know how he was killed.

She admitted suspecting that her husband was a guerrilla since his uncle was known to be one of the leaders of the guerrilla then. She believes that his relation with a leader of the guerrilla was the reason why he was arrested and killed by the Makapilis.

Q.   Do you have any message to Japanese veteran soldiers who are still alive in Japan?

A.   No, I don't. But let me tell you that I cannot forgive the Makapilis who sold my husband to the Japanese. If not for them, he would have survived the Japanese war. Although, I know that it was a Japanese soldier and not the Makapilis who killed my husband. After World War II, I had no choice but to work to feed my family. It was a very hard time to look for a job and so I ended up accepting laundry jobs. Although that was very difficult for me, I kept thinking that if my husband was able to take the sufferings brought by war, my daughter and I will be able to survive this war against poverty.

Q. (To the daughter) Do you have any message to the Japanese people?

A. No, I don't have anything to say to them. Although it was along time ago, I still get affected when I hear stories of the war from my mother.

Q. How about a message to the youths of Japan?

A. No, I don't have any message for them. You know, I have a Japanese friend, but he is not aware of anything that happened to us during the War.

Q. Why haven't you shared your story with your Japanese friend? I'm sure that sharing your story and the pain it caused you and your family will bond you closer together as friends.

A. It's not that easy.

5. **Mr. Juan Gloryoso** (67 years old). He was a guerrilla and a USAFFE veteran. He is now a carpenter and sporting a think beard.

Mr. Gloryoso recalled that when he was captured by the Japanese, he was tortured. He was often beaten and subjected to water torture (i.e., he was forced to continuously drink water without let up until he gagged and vomited). But this did not last, for he was later released after a few days.

Q. Do you still hate the Japanese?

A. No, not anymore since the Japanese was already defeated. Anyway, I was able to survive and that is enough.

Q. What's your opinion on the claim of former war prisoners in Muntinlupa saying that injustice was committed on them during the Manila Trial since they were tried and punished for crimes they did not commit?

A. All Japanese soldiers were guilty. There is no exception. There's not one Japanese soldier who can claim otherwise. They killed and massacred innocent people. If the Japanese Imperial Army did not invade our country, there would not have been suffering, injury, hunger, death, sickness in the country. And so when I was released, a joined the USAFFE to avenge what they did to me in prison.

6. **Mr. Renart Alcantara** (55 years old)

Mr. Alcantara was only seven years old then, so he vaguely remembered the war. However, he recalled that his grandfather was forced by the Japanese to act as mayor of their town. He initially refused the offer since earlier on, the former mayor was killed by the Japanese because he refused to obey orders from them. But there was nothing much he could have done about it and so he was forced to accept the position and be placed in the dilemma where he must show his loyalty to the Japanese at the expense of his Filipino brothers.

Q. What can you say about Japanese soldiers during the War?

A. I was very small then, I don't have much memory of the War and the Japanese soldiers. But I heard a lot of stories about the War from my elders particularly about the bad things the Japanese soldiers did to the Filipino people.

Q. Former Japanese prisoners claim that they were accused of crimes they did not commit and that their trial in Manila was not fair. What can you say about this?

A. Tough luck for them then. I believe that all Japanese soldiers during the war were criminals. They killed innocent Filipinos and ravaged our resources. And If there were a few good Japanese who were kind to the Filipinos, they can be considered part of the aggression. I was told that when the Japanese were "witch-hunting" for guerrillas, all men were asked to line up and the Makapilis were asked to identify members of the guerrillas. But even wrongly identified as guerrillas were brutally executed without any trial. And so, the Japanese does not have the right to claim justice.

Q. But some Japanese war prisoners complained that during their trial, Filipino witnesses arbitrarily accused without proof just any Japanese of participation in the alleged crimes.

A. Really? They complain about that? How could they? When a Japanese soldier was killed by guerrillas then, they gather all residents of the community. If nobody accepts the responsibility of identifying the suspects, out of anger the Japanese killed even innocent civilians without warning. Now, can you say then that they have the right to complain about their trial in Manila? All Japanese soldiers were guilty. During the war, every Filipino, even women and children, hated the Japanese Army because of the cruelty they committed against the Filipino people.

* Unedited English translation of Author's notes.

OTHER WORKS

"Nihonki (Ya Pun Kwai) – Nihongun Senryouka Hongkong Jumin no Senso Taiken" *(Japanese Devil – War Experiences of Hongkong Residents During the Occupation by Japanese Imperial Army)* published by Geridai-Shokun in 1993.

The author gives a detailed documentation of the extent of the havoc wrought by Japanese military occupation of the island of Hongkong, from a macro view of the economy and from the incisive perspective of the inhabitants at that time. In response to the interview conducted by the author, the victims provide lurid accounts of the massive devastation caused by the intruding forces that left them mourning over their lost loved ones.

"Mango no Hana Saku Senjo" *(The Battlefield Under the Full Blossoms of the Mango Tree)* published by Shin-Dokusho-sha in 1995

In this first part of a long novel, the author reveals the brutality and the gory of massacres committed by elements of the Japanese Imperial Army in the Provinces of Laguna and Batangas at the height of World War II. Written from the eyes of Pedro de Guzman, one of the survivors of the February 1945 massacre, a true-to-life story unfolds with shocking revelations and traumatic vividness.

"Beigun ni Tochi wo Ubawareta Okinawajin" *(Okinawan People Robbed of their Own Land by the US Army)* published by Shin-Dokusho-sha in 1997.

The author traces the fate of 60 persons belonging to 10 Japanese families from the time they lost their ancestral lands in the Island of Okinawa due to forcible eviction by the US Army in 1957 up to their migration to Brazil in pursuit of a new beginning. The story is replete with heart-rending accounts by emigres' of their seemingly endless tribulations, lofty dreams and humble entreaty for a quite life.

"Muntinglupa e no Michi" *(The Path to Muntinglupa)* published by Shin-Dokusho-sha in 1997.

In this second part of a long novel, the author tells of the agonizing pain suffered by a former member of the Japanese Imperial Army who was placed behind the bars of War Crime Prison in the Municipality of Muntinglupa after World War II. Pedro de Guzman, a Filipino of a Japanese massacre incident during the war, found himself employed as janitor at the penitentiary. In a juxta positioning of the protagonists, the author brings to fore their innermost anxiety over the immediate future, and their strong biases against each other especially during their encounters inside the prison.

"Batangas no Sora no Shita de" *(Under the Sky of Batangas)* published by Shin-Dokusho-sha in 1998.

In this third part of a long novel, the author revisits Pedro de Guzman and his family 30 years after the war. Due to dire poverty, the de Guzman children were forced to try their luck in Manila but found themselves working in the "entertainment industry" catering primarily to Japanese "sex tourists". The author notes with amusement the fact that Japanese war veterans who visit the Philippines during war memorial services make up the majority of the de Guzman children's clientele.

"Hapon no Fuyu" *(Winter in Japan)* published by Shin-Dokusho-san in 1999.

In this fourth part of a long novel, the author compares the lives of three Filipino Women during winter in Japan. Mary, the eldest daughter of Pedro de Guzman, decides to work in Japan to help provide for her father's medical needs. Her cousin, Cynthia who had an arranged-marriage with a Japanese in Manila, starts a new life in Tohoku area (northern eastern part of Japan). Another cousin. Lilia works as an a-go-go dancer in Japan.

The long novel consists of six parts. At present, Mr. Jintaro Ishida is writing the fifth part tentatively entitled **"Anger at the Seaside"** which will focus on the Batangas Port expansion project, funded by Japanese Overseas Development Assistance (ODA).

INDEX
(INTERVIEWEES)

EPILOGUE

For thousands of Filipino today, the grim memories of the Japanese Occupation are now quite forgotten—a most natural thing to happen because many of us don't value the past as other peoples in our part of the world do.

Westerners, for instance, cannot understand why, on those occasions that we celebrate the fall of Bataan, our streets are decked with Japanese flags as well, and why we have permitted the Japanese to erect shrines and monuments to their dead on Philippines soil.

The atrocities committed by the Imperial Army in this country have been documented again and again, and this is what author Jintaro Ishida does with painstaking labor and fidelity in this landmark book. He recounts his vivid interviews, what he heard and saw. He travelled in Japan and Luzon to talk with Japanese soldiers who were in the Philippines during the war and particularly in 1944 when the massacres occurred in the province of Laguna and Batangas.

Author Ishida's compassion and sincerity are admirable particularly from a Japanese point of view. He dares to ask those taboo questions that demand the most probing and honest replies. In many instances, he gets them thereby, in their totality, they raise several questions about Japanese culture and nationalism.

Why, for instance, in spite of overwhelming evidence, some of the soldiers who were in the Philippines during the period under study refuse to face the truth of what was done to the Filipinos? And why do the Filipinos—particularly their officials—permit these same soldiers to set up shrines for their fallen comrades in a land which they had despoiled? Does the Occupation of the Philippines mean anything to the Filipinos now? And to the Japanese as well? Are the same elements that created barbarity among the Japanese still at work in Japanese society? Is there a continuum in the Japanese character that may erupt in the same kind brutality in the future?

These are, of course, very disturbing questions but for as long as the Japanese like Jintaro Ishida keep confronting their own people with their dark past, it is very possible that the errors of that by gone era may never be repeated. It is in this light that this book—initially published in Japan—has a far deeper value not just to Filipinos but to the Japanese themselves.

Francisco Sionil Jose